From the author of the bestselling *Black Pearls* series comes the first African-American guide to better sex. Beautifully designed and illustrated, *SoulMates* tells you everything you need to know about sex, love, and romance, from the timeless wisdom of the *Kama Sutra* to the latest sexual research.

D I S C O V E R :

What every black person should know about sex

What turns black men and women on . . . in their own words

Sex and love in black folklore—and in the world today

The most romantic couples of all time

Plus tips for

Finding a mate

Setting the mood

Discovering pleasure zones

Deepening spiritual bonds through lovemaking

How to have the best—and healthiest—sex ever

ERIC V. COPAGE is the author of the bestselling *Black Pearls* series of meditation books. He has been a staff editor of the *New York Times Magazine*, a staff reporter for *Life* magazine and the *New York Daily News*, and the music columnist for *Essence* magazine. Mr. Copage has appeared on radio and TV talk shows on CNN and ABC among others. He lives in New Jersey.

SOULMATES

An Illustrated Guide to Black Love, Sex, and Romance

ERIC V. COPAGE

Ⓟ

A PLUME BOOK

PLUME
Published by the Penguin Group
Penguin Putnam Inc., 375 Hudson Street,
New York, New York 10014, U.S.A.
Penguin Books Ltd, 27 Wrights Lane,
London W8 5TZ, England
Penguin Books Australia Ltd, Ringwood,
Victoria, Australia
Penguin Books Canada Ltd, 10 Alcorn Avenue,
Toronto, Ontario, Canada M4V 3B2
Penguin Books (N.Z.) Ltd, 182–190 Wairau Road,
Auckland 10, New Zealand

Penguin Books Ltd, Registered Offices:
Harmondsworth, Middlesex, England

First published by Plume,
a member of Penguin Putnam Inc.

First Printing, September 2001
10   9   8   7   6   5   4   3   2   1

Quotations on pages xi, xvi, 78, 90 are from *The Complete Kama Sutra: The First Unabridged Modern Translation of the Classic Indian Text*. Translated by Alain Daniélou, published by Park Street Press, an imprint of Inner Traditions International, Rochester, VT 05767. Translation copyright © 1994 by Alain Daniélou.

 REGISTERED TRADEMARK — MARCA REGISTRADA

LIBRARY OF CONGRESS CATALOGING-IN-PUBLICATION DATA:
Copage, Eric V.
Soulmates : an illustrated guide to black love, sex, and romance / by Eric V. Copage.
p.   cm.
ISBN 0-452-28159-8
1. Man-woman relationships—United States.   2. Afro-American women—Sexual behavior.
3. Afro-American women—Sexual behavior.   4. Interpersonal communication—United States.
I. Title: Soul mates.   II. Title.
HQ801 .C715 2001
306.7'089'96073—dc21

00-068464

PUBLISHER'S NOTE
The names and identifying characteristics of real people have been changed to protect their pri-
vacy. Every effort has been made to ensure that the information contained in this book is complete and accurate. However, neither the publisher nor the author is engaged in rendering
professional advice or services to the individual reader. The ideas, procedures, and suggestions
contained in this book are not intended as a substitute for consulting with your physician. All
matters regarding your health require medical supervision. Neither the author nor the publisher
shall be liable or responsible for any loss or damage allegedly arising from any information or sug-
gestion in this book.

BOOKS ARE AVAILABLE AT QUANTITY DISCOUNTS WHEN USED TO PROMOTE PRODUCTS OR SERVICES.
FOR INFORMATION PLEASE WRITE TO PREMIUM MARKETING DIVISION, PENGUIN PUTNAM INC., 375
HUDSON STREET, NEW YORK, NEW YORK 10014.

To the incandescence of black love, sex and romance throughout history.
May they continue to light our paths and warm our hearts
until the end of time.

CONTENTS

SOULMATES

Why I Wrote This Book

There is a power that black sexuality
exudes that is as powerful as the
sun shining.

—*Debbie Allen, actress, choreographer*

In the months immediately following my divorce in 1997, I found myself poring over *Cosmopolitan*, *Essence*, *Mademoiselle* and dozens of other women's magazines. I studied the quizzes, scrutinized the round-table conversations, and parsed articles. In an effort to figure out what went wrong with my marriage, I also frequented bookstores, and spent hours thumbing through *Men Are from Mars, Women Are from Venus, What Women and Men Really Want, Love Is a Decision, A Fine Romance,* and other relationship books. Afterward I would plunk down a fat wad of bills at the cash register, and take home my armload of rehabilitative reading.

Next to the self-help books at the stores, I became aware of an ever-expanding number of books about sex. I thumbed through them, and took some home: A tenth-century Chinese treatise called *The Tao of Love, 101 Nights of Grrreat Sex,* an illustrated book of Tantric sex, an illustrated edition of the Arabian classic on love, *The Perfumed Garden,* the Kinsey Report, *The Art of Kissing,* and several of the many editions of the Indian sex classic, the *Kama Sutra.*

From the "Master of the Cave Profound" I learned Chinese nicknames for penis (Jade Stalk, Male Vanguard), clitoris (the Mouse in the Empty Boat) and vagina (Jade Gate). From the *Kama Sutra* I learned about the art of tattooing with my teeth the Line of Jewels, the Broken Cloud, and the Bite of the Boar on the rose-petal-soft skin of my beloved. I learned about making marks with my nails—a Peacock's Foot, the Leaf of the Blue Lotus. I learned when to emit the sounds Phut! Phat! and the thundering sound. From other books I learned about different positions for sexual intercourse: the Rear Flying Wild Duck, the Screw of Archimedes, Splitting the Bamboo, the Arch of the Rainbow. I learned about leather and fur-lined manacles, ostrich feathers, and black satin blindfolds.

But what I learned most of all after viewing hundreds of pictures and drawings in scores of books is that black men, women, and couples were very rarely depicted in sex books. In fact, at that time, I remember no black couples, and the few black men and women I saw were usually so light skinned that I had to double-check that they were indeed black. In hundreds of pages of text rarely did I read about black feelings and attitudes about erotic love and sex, and the value we put on them. And while that has changed somewhat in the past year or so, I still find myself yearning for a book that celebrates black love with photographs or drawings that are sensuous and tantalizing, yet at the same time instructive—a how-to manual, if you will. The purpose, however, would not be to reduce the physical aspects of love to series of soulless exercises, or sexual calisthenics. On a physical level the idea is to provide a manual of technique, like the exercises a pianist or a dancer learns, so that mastery of their instrument becomes second nature, and they can rise above technique. On a romantic and emotional level the idea is to provide guidance and signposts in anticipation of the inspirational moment.

In preparation to write *SoulMates* I surveyed over four hundred (most of the respondents, over two thirds, were women) black people, a few from Africa and the Caribbean, but most of them American. But don't think I am trying to emulate Masters and Johnson, *The Hite Report,* or *The Janus Report.* I am not trying to out-Kinsey Kinsey. This book is not meant to be academic or scientific. The purpose is to give our people—black people—a much-needed voice, and a place for the collective memories, words or wisdom, and folklore about expressions of our lives on the most intimate emotional, spiritual, and physical level.

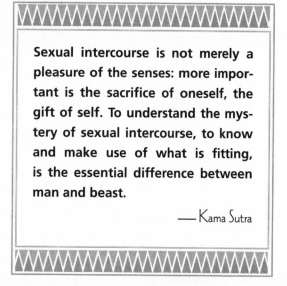

> Sexual intercourse is not merely a pleasure of the senses: more important is the sacrifice of oneself, the gift of self. To understand the mystery of sexual intercourse, to know and make use of what is fitting, is the essential difference between man and beast.
>
> —Kama Sutra

On one level my models are the Japanese pillow books, or the many marriage manuals from around the world. And as the armature to *SoulMates* I have used the *Kama Sutra,* the two-thousand-year-old Indian treatise on love. When the words *Kama Sutra* are pronounced, visions of sexual positions worthy of a circus contortionist frequently spring to mind. But if you actually read the *Kama Sutra,* you see that it regards the physical aspects of making love as only one part to making a well-rounded person and a sound relationship. In this book, like the *Kama Sutra,* I try to address those larger issues. But this time the love and larger issues chronicled and celebrated are ours. And the book includes, I hope, information distant future generations will cherish about black love, black romance, and the physical aspects of sex among those of African descent. It aims to have information relevant to those on the cusp of adulthood, those about to enter into the commitment of a long-term relationship, or those celebrating the anniversary of an existing relationship.

In this volume I have included commentary from everyday black people about sex. The comments by everyday black people are important because our relationship with sex is couples, owing to our unique history in this country that has reduced our sexuality to stereotypes. Many of us find ourselves subliminally either trying to live up to the myth of the hypersexed black man or woman, or live it down.

This book is about the healthy expression of our sexual selves. This book regards good sex, romance, and love as aspects of life at its most intense and satisfying, an inner journey—built, ultimately, for two—of discovery. This book deals with the whole range of man-woman relationships in life—from finding a mate to developing a relationship, to sustaining that relationship. As for sex, it deals with mood, grooming, seduction, sexual union, postcoital behavior, and our folklore and contemporary experiences, as well as positions for sexual intercourse.

My philosophy, echoing that of the *Kama Sutra*, among other books on sex, is that sexual relations are one pillar of any long-term relationship. This book is harmonious with my other books, *Kwanzaa: An African-American Celebration of Culture and Cooking*, my best-selling *Black Pearls* meditation series, my novella *Kwanzaa Fable*, and my book *Soul Food: Inspirational Stories for African Americans*, in that they ask a fundamental question: What is a black man or woman? The answer, based on observation of great black men and women of today and throughout history is—to be a black person is not merely a matter of color, but a conscious choice. And that choice is not just harmonious with, but mandates having, a strong moral core, and an eager embrace of the good and the beautiful in this world.

SOULMATES

What every black person should know about sex

That sex is more than just the bump and grind.   Richard, 30

666

Sex is an expression and it isn't always the quantity or length of time, but the quality, the preparation. Be gentle.   Sharon, 43

666

Pay attention! Your partner's body will tell you almost everything you need to know. And if it doesn't, don't be afraid to ask.   Theresa, 27

666

Don't ask for what you would not return. Say no if you really don't want a certain thing. Don't use guilt to make a person do your will. Louise, 50

666

Women should become familiar with their bodies. They need to know that masturbation isn't taboo.   Sarah, 30

666

To be sensitive to and considerate of each other's needs, emotionally, physically, mentally, and spiritually.   Samuel, 40

666

To respect their own bodies. If they do that, they will respect the body of others.   Lucy, 46

666

Men need to know that women are not built like they are sexually. We need foreplay. And a lot of it, for a very good lovemaking session. Also, men who practice oral sex need to know that there is a point when women are beyond being sexually aroused and peaked. Please stop when we say so.   Jacki, 37

Like most things in life, giving always means you'll get in return. Bella, 26

How to relax. Go with the flow. Be open minded.   Alma, 42

Techniques and taking their time.   Michelle, 29

To do what comes natural with no limits.   Isaac, 44

How to make your partner come back for more.   Battina, 23

Care about the person. You can have detached sex, but connected sex is far more enjoyable.   Jesse, 27

To find out what their partner really needs from them, as well as what they really want from their partner.   Rose, 38

Many believe that a couple has no need to learn erotic arts, and that nature will teach them everything. Those who believe that, on reaching middle age, become unhappy and desperate. Their life in common no longer has any savor and mutual hostility develops. Vatsayayana explains how, in order to guard against such a change, the preliminaries of copulation can be used, kisses and caresses that awaken desire, and, when amorous stimulation has reached its peak, continuing immediately with kisses, scratchings, and so on.

—Kama Sutra

What do you wish someone had told you before your first sexual experience?

That the first time you do not see stars; the first time I couldn't understand what all the hype was about.   Linda, 24

666

To do it for love, with someone you love. It would have meant more. Nicole, 39

666

I wish someone had told me that an orgasm for a woman is not as easy as the Danielle Steele books made it seem.   Rose, 38

666

I wish someone had told me to wait even longer. The first couple of times weren't worth it.   Carol, 36

666

How to have an orgasm every time, because unfortunately until recently, I did not even know that women came, at least physically.   Diane, 25

666

Sex starts in the mind. Don't just jump to the act itself. Always insist on great, innovative foreplay. I think it gives more value to the total experience.   Katherine, 31

666

I wish someone had told me about orgasm. I didn't know I was supposed to feel them.   Susan, 42

666

That it does not have to hurt. If I had been told that, I would have found out how it could have been more enjoyable, rather than thinking it's going to hurt the first few times, then it'll get good.   Claudia, 30

※※※

Not to masturbate often because it increases your chance of ejaculating too soon. The brain stem is used to instant gratification with masturbation, and with a vagina reacts twice as fast.   Arthur, 30

※※※

That it was more than just sex and that nine times out of ten your first time is horrible, and that a man's perception of sex is totally different than a woman's. If I had more understanding, I think I would have waited longer and my expectations would have been different.   Nia, 26

※※※

The smells, the wetness. Preparation for the reality of the physical contact, not just the romantic aspects.   William, 38

※※※

That it is not nasty. There has been a lot of guilt, even with my husband, because of the way older people spoke of sex. They made it seem awful and sinful. It took me a long time to get those thoughts out of my head.
Annette, 50

※※※

That it was going to most likely be painful. I wish someone would have told me so that I would have been prepared.   Cindy, 30

※※※

Not to do it with another virgin.   Patty, 23

※※※

To go slower, so I could have relished it.   Dana, 29

I wish someone other than my mother told me sex would be better in an appropriate level of development in a committed/married relationship, in love and friendship instead of in lust alone at age fifteen. Samuel, 33

❧

The importance of feelings that go with sexual relationships. I wish that, because I would not have wasted so much time in meaningless sexual relationships.   Florence, 46

❧

That there is more to it than penetration . . . then I would not have wasted all those years thinking that something was wrong with me, because I couldn't understand how women could get any kind of pleasure in just being pounded by a man. My first experience was just that: a man—my college boyfriend—just on top of me grinding. No foreplay. No nothing. It was awful.   Gina, 37

❧

That it was going to change my whole life. I would have done things differently. Would have waited.   Ruby, 25

In the Name
of Love

INCANTATION

The *Kama Sutra* begins with the supposition that there are three important things in life: *dharma,* or spiritual discipline; *artha,* learning how to master the material world by accumulating money and other symbols of worldly success; and *kama,* the enjoyment of beauty and pleasure.

In contemporary terms the *Kama Sutra* model suggests that whether we are Christian, Moslem, Buddhist, or Jew, or whether we pay homage to the ancient gods of our ancestors, we should strive to pay attention not just to the letter but to the spirit of our chosen faith, and we should attend to that spiritual devotion every minute of every day.

For those of us of African descent there is another level, a level best summarized with a much-discredited phrase, *to be a credit to our race*. Too often that phrase has been interpreted as kowtowing to white people, striving to make them comfortable by not being too loud or too assertive. It's debatable whether that was ever a black definition of *credit to our race*. Regardless, let us now, in the name of LOVE, define it as striving to do the very best we can in whatever endeavor we face.

In the name of LOVE let it mean striving to live up to our full spiritual potential. Sure, it's nice if we know the proper way to spoon soup or the proper order to use the silverware at a formal dinner. Such social graces help us to be comfortable in public. But there are etiquette books for that. So, in the name of LOVE for our ancestors, for their commitment, for their sacrifice and faith, let us commit ourselves to seeking out the good in life. We can acknowledge bad days. We don't have to go through life with a moronic "smiley"-face grin pasted on our face. We need not pretend disappointments do not exist. But in the name of LOVE let us realize that while brooding on our setbacks we passed a park that was incandescent with flowers. Let us not be blind to rosy-fingered dawns.

In the name of our ancestors and in the name of LOVE let us pledge to make the world a better place for our passing through it. This is not a new concept. Codified by Dr. Maulana Karenga as the fifth principle of Kwanzaa, Kuumba or creativity—"to do always as much as we can, in whatever way we can, in order to leave our community more beautiful and beneficial than we inherited it"—this is an oath black men and women have taken since we drew our very first breath on this planet. It is this oath that informed the actions of Martin Luther King, Jr., Malcolm X, Rosa Parks, Fannie Lou Hamer, and Toussaint-Louverture, as well as the thousands of local heroes over the centuries who have adopted an orphaned black child, provided a stop on the underground railroad at great personal risk, or volunteered to take time from their busy life to oversee a midnight basketball program.

In the name of LOVE let us recognize, but not be overcome by, the material riches of this world. Let us recognize that a well-rounded twenty-first-century black man and woman must understand, if not embrace, how money and power work in this world. For those who are eager to participate in capitalism, let us pursue the many books—including those targeted to the unique needs of black Americans—that teach about the importance of savings and how to invest wisely and in a way that maximizes our political power.

In the name of LOVE let us pledge ourselves to Muscular Black Pride and do simple concrete things each and every day to affirm ourselves and our heritage. In the name of LOVE let us pledge to take steps to make a better world not next year, not next month, not next week or tomorrow, but today. This very moment.

In the name of LOVE let us have the courage to dream and let us have the solidarity to encourage the dreams of others. Let us have the wisdom to recognize that the fighting spirit of our ancestors is all around us—sitting beside us on a bus; standing in front of us at a movie ticket booth—looking back at us in the reflection of a department store window.

In the name of LOVE let us remember the sacrifices of our ancestors, the splintered families, the loss of jobs, loss of health, and even loss of life. Let us remember that our ancestors made those sacrifices in the hope of blazing a path to a Golden Age of Prosperity for our people. Let us not let them down.

In the name of LOVE let us honor our ancestors' memory and sacrifices by continuing to strive, and to struggle with our head held high with pride as we work toward that Golden Age. In the name of LOVE let us have the courage to make mistakes.

In the name of LOVE let us have the compassion to forgive the mistakes of others. Let us have the curiosity to read and listen, and the intelligence to analyze what we've read and heard. Let us remember to question.

In the name of LOVE let us pledge to proper exercise and diet so that we have the energy to accomplish our goals as individuals and as a people. Let us pledge to proper exercise and diet so that we can live long, healthy lives and enjoy our prosperity after achieving our goals.

In the name of LOVE let us remember to speak up. In the name of LOVE let us remember to stand up. And let us, in the name of LOVE, have the strength not just to endure, but to celebrate this precious gift provided to us from the loins and wombs of our ancestors. In the name of LOVE let us celebrate life.

The most romantic couples of all time

James and Florida Evans from *Good Times*. Through all the fighting and struggling, they still managed to hug, kiss, or dance every few episodes. Tony, 30

Shango, the Yoruba god of thunder and procreation, and his wife, Oya, the warrior goddess of the wind, which represents fate, and the market-place, as well as the cemetery and death. I like the elemental powers the two represent. I mean, how much more basic can you get—having power over birth and death. The couple symbolizes the power of black people to me.   Paul, 30

Whitley and Dwayne from *A Different World*. The writers made the characters have totally different backgrounds, interests, and goals, yet they showed how it could work out. I know this is TV, but it does give us couples that are mismatched a way of dealing with our differences. Dawn, 26

Holly and Rodney Peete. They are so in love and they got busy having their family quick. He proposed on national television. I just love seeing two people in love and seeing them share that love with children. Henrietta, 50

⑥⑥⑥

Tea Cake and the sister in *Their Eyes Were Watching God*. They were kinda like these rebels for their time, and seemed to be living life to its fullest to the very end. Regina, 22

⑥⑥⑥

Ruby Dee and Ossie Davis because they have a deep friendship and respect for one another and have collaborated well with each other. The relationship wasn't for frivolous reasons. John, 35

⑥⑥⑥

Denzel and Paula Washington because they appear to be a happy and well-adjusted married couple. Sylvia, 46

⑥⑥⑥

Will Smith and Jada Pinkett. They represent the current generation, and give us all hope that people in their late twenties or early thirties can be in love the old-fashioned way. I love the way they support each other. Toni, 37

⑥⑥⑥

Lauryn Hill and Bob Marley's son seem like a for-real couple—loving and understanding of each other's careers. Charlotte, 37

⑥⑥⑥

Oprah and Steadman—the way he looks at her and the way she talks about her "steady." Dorothy, 29

⑥⑥⑥

Essence editor Susan Taylor and her husband. They seem to have each other's back.   Sally, 42

❧❧❧

The Huxtables. There are times to be romantic even with children around. They showed that people can have a family and still keep the romance going.   Carolyn, 36

❧❧❧

General Colin Powell and his wife. They seem to be in love and have a sparkle in their eyes.   Gwen, 28

❧❧❧

Camille and Bill Cosby. They have persevered through good and bad times, and hung together in their time of great tragedy and when his daughter from another relationship surfaced after many years. Nessa, 28

The *Kama Sutra* suggests that a completely grounded and well-rounded individual be knowledgeable in the arts and sciences. While a complete knowledge or even a semicomplete knowledge for the average individual may not be practical or possible in the twenty-first century—after all, the world has become a bit more complicated over the two thousand years since the great Hindu love text was compiled and written—we can still aspire to read books, newspapers, and magazines and to have intelligent conversations about them either face to face or over the Internet. We can look at films and television intelligently—critically. We can be regular visitors to concert halls and museums. We can write poems or create drawings for personal expression—to give vent to a troubling emotion, or to crystallize something wonderful that happened in our lives. We can create sketches, paintings, snatches of prose, or bellow out sentimental melodies in a joyful voice. And *joyful* is the key word, for these expressions needn't rival Whitney Houston or Marvin Gaye. In these instances of joyful baying and joyful scribbling, it really is the thought that matters.

Khalil of Atlanta, Georgia, tells the story of how he picked up the piano after not playing it for almost twenty years. "My hands had all the grace of an arthritis sufferer," he said. "And it's not like I was ever terrific, even in high school and college when I performed in R and B bands. But I fell in love with this woman and it was something we could do together. Something to share. We sang old Motown tunes from the sixties. I sounded like a cat in a room full of rocking chairs, and she, if anything, sounded worse. But we had fun. It was a really spiritual coming together, even if it did have dogs and cats howling and screeching for miles around!"

Michael of Oakland, California, says he was never an artist, and never had any facility with his hands. "I can't draw worth anything. But I really loved this woman, so I made her a mobile. I went to a museum store and got a children's mobile kit for a couple of bucks. Then I went to a stationery store and got some yellow construction paper. I cut out about nine three-inch circles. On one side of six of the circles I drew a smiling "smiley" face; on the remaining circles I drew frowning "smiley" faces. On the back of the smiling faces I simply wrote *With you* and on the frowning faces wrote *Without you*. I felt foolish giving such a goofy present. Very amateurish, I thought. But it was a sincere expression of how I felt about her. It turns out, she liked it."

Monica of Shaker Heights, Ohio, said: "After about six months into our relationship this guy I was seeing gave me this little, well, I suppose you would call it a poem. I still have it:

I wanna hold your hand

I wanna nibble your fingers

I wanna watch you walk

I wanna caress your thighs

I wanna hear your voice

I wanna nuzzle your neck

I wanna smell your hair

I wanna devour your lips

I wanna rub your feet

I wanna kiss your breasts

I wanna look into your eyes

I wanna delight in your sex

"What I liked about it is that it showed some effort and that he was thinking about me," Monica continued. "It showed an appreciation of me that was at once gentle and ravenous."

Another arrow the *Kama Sutra* says every person should have in their moral quiver is that of being a good citizen. In the *Kama Sutra* this meant "holding festivals in honor of different deities, social gatherings, drinking parties, picnics. . . ." But for the twenty-first-century black man or woman, the activities of the "citizen," must be wholly redefined. In these complicated times, when everyone has a different idea of what doing the right thing is, it is difficult to dictate one true way to be a good citizen. A good starting point might be summed up by saying to be of service to the black community. Volunteering for tutoring or after-school basketball leagues would be a good start. So might finding something to compliment on the random black child you see, or perhaps offering encouragement and positive feelings to a friend. And, I might add, improving the black community and its citizenry is improving all of America whether that is the intent or not. In its most distilled phrasing, being a good African American citizen means living up to his or her potential to exert some positive influence on a daily basis.

Alice, who lives in a Cleveland suburb, said she is an active member of the PTA of her children's elementary school, which is thirty-five percent or so African American.

"You know the saying," said the mother of twin ten-year-old boys. " 'You've got to be in it to win it.' There are times I would prefer not to drag myself to someone's house or to the school auditorium after a day at the office. There are times, even with my husband's help with dinner, laundry, and so forth, when I would prefer to put my feet up and not hold a meeting at my house about how to get funds to get more equipment for our science lab. But I found out from my own growing up in a so-called integrated neighborhood that you can't just assume that because you are living somewhere that you will be treated as an equal, that your children are getting what they need, and what they deserve. Plus, it is just a part of being a good neighbor, an active member and positive member of the community. In short, a good citizen."

Graham, a young lawyer who lives in Dallas, said one way he exhibits good citizenship is by being active in politics.

"Some people get upset that I am a Republican," said Graham from the air-conditioned, glassed-in porch of his modest but comfortable home. "But I believe in their stated message about the place of government and capitalism. That doesn't mean I am less proud of my heritage, my 'race.' Besides, I think it is wise for us to play across the political spectrum, according to our beliefs. That's what corporate campaign contributors do—they spread their bet in supporting political candidates. That way, no matter who comes out on top, someone will owe them."

Is sex important for a long-term relationship?

Yes. However, I feel the real power is in the romance and the giving and receiving of attention.   Edward, 30

ⓖⓖⓖ

Sex gives you a way of bonding on a different level.   Gladys, 26

ⓖⓖⓖ

I think sex is important as you continue your relationship because it's the joy of just being intimate with each other no matter how old you are. Maria, 43

ⓖⓖⓖ

Gotta keep up both the sex and the romance, that's what makes the relationship different from "just friends."   William, 38

ⓖⓖⓖ

Affection in general is more important overall.   Maura, 27

ⓖⓖⓖ

If sex is not possible because of illness, there should be some way to show how you feel either orally or through hugging and touching. Never, though, should a person go elsewhere for sex. Be true to that partner.   Grace, 50

ⓖⓖⓖ

Sex should add to what the couple already shares.   Patty, 23

ⓖⓖⓖ

Sex is important in any relationship as a way of showing total and complete unabandoned feelings. Not the whipped-cream, tie-me-up, tie-me-down sex, but the sex that brings to the surface the love you feel inside for your partner. Toni, 46

You have to have the same sexual wants and needs. If you don't, it can cause problems.   Belle, 26

⊚⊚⊚

If I please my husband and if he pleases me, the chances of either one of us cheating is lower.   Ellen, 29.

⊚⊚⊚

Love, communication, and trust are well ahead of it. Sex is important, but not number one.   Susan, 42

⊚⊚⊚

Sex is the dessert. Sex helps to relieve stress and at the same time connect intimately with the one you love.   Nancy, 33

⊚⊚⊚

I do not think the importance of it diminishes, but that people tend to take each other for granted and forget about keeping the spark alive in a relationship. It's bad when we lose focus as to what helped us come together in the first place, and sex was one of those things.   Alice, 50

⊚⊚⊚

Sex is one of the things that got us to this point in terms of the longevity and relating to each other in a manner that is unique and special to us. Rose, 38

⊚⊚⊚

Sex is very much a big part of any intimate relationship. But it also has everything to do with intimacy and touching one another in places that the body can never reach.   Michael, 30

Welcome to the Pleasure Zones

GETTING TO KNOW YOUR STUFF

Before we get busy, we should get familiar, familiar with the basic mechanics of male and female genital function and construction. Men might have a greater familiarity with their penis because it is so—out there! But women might want to shutter the windows, lock the doors, and take an hour or so with a mirror to get familiar with their intimate parts. . . .

Brothas

The Penis

Is there a part of the human anatomy more fraught with symbolism? About which we are more anxious? Not even breasts come close. And there are two of them! Look around, and you'll see penises everywhere: a train going through a tunnel, the Sears Tower, a corporate takeover struggle, a magician's wand. It is symbolic of power and the lack of it. And it has a huge racial symbolism. But fortunately or unfortunately, there are no reliable studies to attest that black men, on average, really have bigger erect penises than men of other races. There is, however, some evidence that black men are longer when flaccid, which may contribute to the myth that they are bigger when erect, also. Like Eskimos and snow, the men are very familiar with their penis, and therefore there have accumulated many names for it. Here is a sampler:

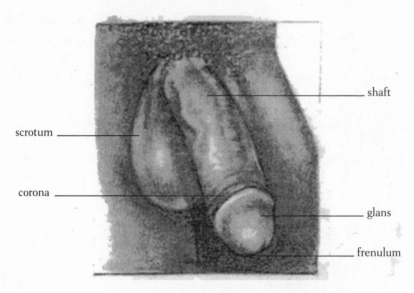

scrotum

corona

shaft

glans

frenulum

Just me and my . . . penis, stick, dick, pole, love jockey, peter, ding-ding, snake, protein injector, black monster, pussy tamer, johnson, bone, piece, woody, Mr. Pokey, ding, jimmy, buddy, rod, cock, nailer, stuffer, love bone, buddy, jewels, thang, stuff, joy stick . . .

Yet, a penis by any other name would still be comprised of its suite of parts. The longest section is the **shaft;** the bulbous part at the top of the shaft is the **head** or **glans;** the V-shaped notch on the underside of the head is the **frenulum;** the ridge area between the head and shaft is the **corona.** The head, corona, and frenulum are loaded with nerve endings, and are usually the most sensitive parts of the penis. But let us not forget the other regions of male sexual anatomy. There is: The **scrotum,** the sac hanging underneath the penis. The scrotum holds two **testicles** (also called testes). They average one and three quarters to two inches long, and an inch wide. They are usually a little asymmetrical, one (usually the left) hanging lower than the other. Testicles manufacture sperm (the stuff men use to make babies) and male hormones called androgens, mainly testosterone. Each testicle makes almost 150 million sperm each day. Why are the testicles just hanging around out there? Because the

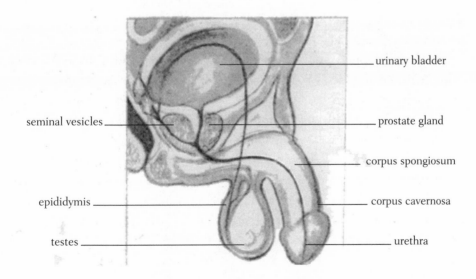

seminal vesicles _____
epididymis _____
testes _____

_____ urinary bladder
_____ prostate gland
_____ corpus spongiosum
_____ corpus cavernosa
_____ urethra

optimal temperature for sperm production is two to three degrees Fahrenheit lower than body temperature. That's one reason why when there is a problem with male fertility, doctors may recommend that the man wear boxer shorts rather than jockey style. The extra distance from his body (i.e., lower temperature) can facilitate sperm production. The testicles are sensitive to any temperature change—due to the weather, sexual arousal, or exercise. Muscles in the scrotum and testicles expand and contract, lowering and raising the testicles to regulate their heat. You don't believe me? Just jump in a cold shower and take a look.

We've all heard about the **prostate** gland, mainly as something that will give a significant number of men problems as they age. (That is why every man beginning at age forty should have an annual prostate exam.) The prostate, a one-and-a-half-inch-long chestnut-shaped organ beneath the bladder, is reachable by inserting a finger into the anus. The prostate is sometimes called the male "G-spot" because of the erotic pleasure some men, including heterosexual men, can derive from having it massaged. (Others have an irrepressible need to urinate, if not outright pain.) If you don't want your girlfriend probing you there, yet are in an experimental mood, try having her rub your perineum, located between the scrotum and the anus. A gentle touching there, especially near orgasm, can put pressure on the prostate. Then you can discover whether prostate manipulation is your cup of tea. The prostate and the glands located underneath them, a pair of pea-sized organs called **Cowper's glands,** create fluids in which sperm is transported. But the bulk of the seminal fluid in which sperm is carried is created in the two **seminal vesicles,** located just above the prostate. The **vas deferens** carries sperm from the **epididymis** (tubes located on the back side of the testicles, where sperm cool their heels until ejaculation), into the **urethra,** located inside the penis shaft (the urethra culminates in the "pee hole" of your penis). The urethra carries both urine and semen out of the penis, but a valve inside the **urinary bladder** prevents the two substances from going through the urethra at the same time.

Male Sexual Response

Now that we've named the parts of the male sexual apparatus, and examined them, let's see how the whole process works. There are three steps in male sexual arousal: desire, arousal, and orgasm. Desire is emotion. Horniness, you might say. It is seeing your girlfriend innocently walking that walk of hers down a grocery aisle and wanting to take her then and there. Some say that desire arises solely from emotion. Others contend that it is a result of hormonal changes. Whatever the root cause, it transforms itself rather seamlessly into arousal, the second step. Some men need a lot of physical stimulation for arousal, others virtually none. Physiologically, erection occurs when the spongy erectile tissue of the penis—the two **corpus cavernosa,** which run along either side of the penis and underneath it, and the **corpus spongiosum,** which surrounds the urethra—become engorged with blood, making the penis stiff. Simultaneously, the scrotum shrinks, bringing the testicles up closer to the body, as the prostate gland swells. The excitement intensifies, either through manual manipulation or the thrusting of intercourse. Nearly two thirds of men get erect nipples during arousal. Breathing becomes heavy, and eventually there is orgasm and ejaculation. Like a wave receding back into the sea, the excitement and erection subside (the refractory phase), and the man's body slowly returns to normal. Whether and how soon a man can have another erection is determined by his age, health, constitution, and energy level at the time.

Sistahs

The Vulva

At first glance the vulva, the external sex organs of a woman, seems less mythologized and freighted with symbolism than the penis. This appears to be the case for two reasons. First, the vulva is seldom seen—tucked up, as it were, between the thighs—whereas a man's genitalia are hard to hide, dangling in front of him like a lantern. Consequently, men are sometimes more familiar with the appearance of their own genitalia, while women's remain a mystery. To take away the mystery, and to increase the pleasure that might be derived from the vulva, many women find it useful to take a hand-held mirror and a flashlight to examine themselves. A woman secrets herself somewhere where she will not be disturbed and pulls her lips apart, wonders at the size of her clitoris, and marvels at the color of the upper part of the vaginal canal. The examination may or may not lead to masturbation. If it does, so much the better, because it is the consensus among sex experts that through masturbation, men and women—but *especially* women—can learn what turns them on: how they like to be touched and where. This knowledge improves her sex life with her significant other. Sometimes, if both parties are comfortable and relaxed enough, the couple can use the mirror and embark on an investigation together. Even though the man has a better vantage point from which to view his partner's private parts, it is unlikely that he has ever done it. It is probably as much an enigma to him as it is to her. The playful and instructive exploration they do together can become a sensual experience.

The second reason the vulva is not as fraught with symbolism as the penis is that the vulva is the repository of not just two meanings—aggression or

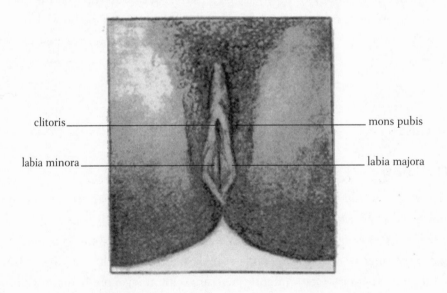

clitoris ———————————————————— mons pubis

labia minora ———————————————————— labia majora

impotence—but a crazy quilt of symbology, fears, and expectations. Why? One reason is that the vulva is actually a collection of genitalia, a place rather than thing. It, or one of its constituent parts, can be a symbol of comfort, of returning to the womb, of warmth and safety, of ecstatic pleasure. It can be a symbol of terror—*vagina dentata,* the vagina full of teeth that devours all who dare approach its maw. The vulva can be the object of revulsion or bewilderment because of its taste, its secretions, and its monthly riverlet of blood. It can be a symbol of mystery. It brings forth life. It gives unearthly pleasure, hinted at with an aroma that can quicken the pulse. It is hidden, even from—make that especially from—its owner, who cannot view it directly. Not surprisingly, the vulva, like the penis, has a host of nicknames, some endearing, some jocular, some whorish and naughty. Here are a few:

Travels with my . . . vagina, pussy, black hole, bush, nookie, crack, water hole, twat, cookie, crotch, fist, bubblegum, honeypot, gash, wet spot, lower lips, the Y, nana, coco, pumpum, coochie, Mrs. Brownstone, cooch, cho-cho, cunt, gate, joy juice, love canal, cathouse, punanny, box, stuff, peach, snatch . . .

*   *   *

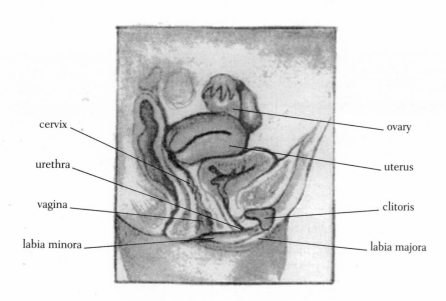

cervix

urethra

vagina

labia minora

ovary

uterus

clitoris

labia majora

The **mons pubis** (also called mons veneris, mount of Venus, and mons), is a soft, fleshy mound covered with pubic hair that rests above the vulva, almost protectively. In fact, the entire area seems protected to the nines, and the person exploring its mysteries has to push aside shroud after shroud, veil after veil. There are the **labia majora** (the outer lips), two folds of skin that act as sentinels to protect the other, inner genitals. These outer lips vary in size and shape, depending on the woman. Their exterior is first covered with hair during puberty; their interior is satiny. Parting the labia majora, you will find the **labia minora** (the inner lips).

Far from fleshy and hairy, these lips, about an inch and a half in length, are hairless and reminiscent, in their wavy shape and thinness, of the petals of carnations, violets, or roses. Like the outer lips the labia minora are characterized by a great variety of shape and color depending on the woman. Beyond the labia minora is yet another veil to peer under—the **hood of the clitoris,** which lies over the **clitoris,** the only organ in the human body exclusively for sexual pleasure. It is small, an inch or so depending on the woman, although most of it is embedded in the soft tissue surrounding it.

The clitoris is densely packed with nerve endings, which make it an extremely sensitive spot. Some think of the clitoris as a minipenis. (Or of the penis as a gargantuan clitoris!) In structure, certainly the two are similar. The clitoris is comprised of a **glans** (head) and a **shaft** (body), although only the head is directly visible. Like the penis on a man, the clitoris can vary in size depending on the woman. Like the penis, the clitoris has two **corpora cavernosa,** masses of spongy erectile tissue on either side of the shaft that swell during sexual arousal and create a minierection. Clitoral stimulation is usually necessary to achieve orgasm.

Right below the clitoris is the urinary opening, the **urethra,** through which women urinate. It is not a sex organ. Below the urethra is what all the fuss is about, at least as far as most men are concerned, the **vaginal opening,** the entranceway to the vagina and the internal reproductive organs.

*   *   *

The **vagina,** which means "sheath" in Latin, is the expandable and collapsible tube that connects the vaginal opening with the **cervix,** the opening of the **uterus** (or womb). The vagina is the conduit for menstrual blood and babies. It is also a receptacle for the penis during intercourse. Only three to five inches long, the vagina will lengthen during the course of sexual excitement to accommodate the penis. (Which is not to say that the longer the penis the better; the most sensitive part of the vagina, the part with the greatest number of nerve endings, is the first third or so near the vaginal opening.) A healthy vagina is always a little moist, the degree of which depends on where a women is in her menstrual cycle and her level of sexual excitement. The natural moisture of the vagina helps keep it healthy, and women should be careful not to harm those natural infection-fighting secretions if they use deodorants or douches.

The **os** is the tiny indentation in the middle of the cervix, or opening to the vagina. During childbirth the cervix expands enough to let the baby pass through. The os blocks objects such as a finger or tampon or penis from entering the uterus. But the os is permeable to menstrual blood and sperm.

The **uterus** is shaped like an inverted pear and is located near the bottom of the abdomen. The uterus is where the baby develops. It expands up to twenty-four times in size as the baby grows, and is equipped with muscles that rhythmically contract to push the baby out during childbirth. The uterine lining, the **endometrium,** is what helps nourish a fetus.

The two tubes that extend from the top of the uterus in either direction to the ovaries are called **Fallopian tubes.** They are about four inches long, and their ends resemble daisies or sunflowers. The ends of the tubes surround, rather than attach to, the **ovaries,** the pair of women's sex organs each about the size of an almond. The ovaries produce the female sex hormones, estrogen and progesterone, and store and release eggs.

The eggs are stored in little pockets called follicles. In a woman's childbearing years the follicles release one ripe egg per month. This is called ovulation. Each month after ovulation the Fallopian tubes carry the eggs from the ovary to the uterus, or womb, a pear-shaped organ in which the fertilized egg is nourished until it becomes a child ready to be delivered. When there is no

Playin' It Safe(r)

While this book is directed primarily toward couples involved in long-term relationships, we also realize that it can take time to find that special, perfect someone. In the meantime, if you engage in sexual relations, it should be safe(r) sex, which means sex that doesn't involve exchanges of body fluids into mouth or anus, and into the vagina for a woman or the urethra for a man. You should also not touch sores that are caused by STIs (sexually transmitted infections) or STDs (sexually transmitted diseases) and of course not have sex if you have such sores. If you are sexually active and non-monogamous, you should get checked for STDs annually.

When people think about the dangers of unsafe sex, the specters of HIV infection and AIDS most frequently come to mind. While it is true that you can die from AIDS, the other diseases spread through sexual contact— genital warts, genital herpes, hepatitis B, chlamydia, syphilis, gonorrhea among them—should not be taken lightly. Some have no cure, while others, if not caught in time, can cause sterility, or diseases that will debilitate you for life. You can also get run of the mill illnesses such as cold, flu, and mononucleosis through sexual contact.

Some STDs are spread through unprotected vaginal or anal sex, others through unprotected oral sex. The key word here is *unprotected* and the question is, What equals protection? Sponges, diaphragms, spermicide,

Norplant, or the Pill won't prevent you from getting an STD. The 100 percent solution for safe sex is masturbation. Barring that, there is a progression of intimate contact—sensual massage, sex toys, fantasy play—that can be explored.

If you are going to have oral sex or intercourse, the most effective way to prevent getting a disease is to use a condom, either the male or female variety (but not both together). Another measure you can take is the dental dam, a six-inch square piece of latex that can be purchased in dental and medical supply stores for protection if you engage in cunnilingus or analingus. (Wash off the talc before using it.) You can make your own dental dam by cutting a rolled non-spermicidal latex condom. When you unroll it, you will have dental dam–like protection, although the material will be much thinner. Some people claim to have used a square of cellophane to the same effect. The most important thing to remember about the male condom is put it on carefully so that it won't break (don't pull it tight against the head of the penis; leave a little pocket for the semen); also, withdraw the penis carefully so that no semen is lost. Use the condom *only* with water-based lubricants. Never use with oil-based lubricants such as Vaseline or massage oil: they will destroy the condom. For more information on safer sex, check out the Planned Parenthood website (www.plannedparenthood.com), which is authoritative, thorough, and engaging.

fertilization, a layer of the uterus, along with the egg, is shed monthly during menstruation.

Each ovary contains about four hundred thousand eggs, the lifetime supply for the woman. That is more than enough, however, since women on average release only about four hundred to five hundred eggs during the childbearing years. In middle age most women stop menstruating and enter menopause, and the ovaries gradually shut down and shrink to the size of a pea.

Female Sexual Response

On certain levels men and women are alike. Their sexual responses have the same number of stages. They both begin with desire (possibly psychological, possibly hormonal, possibly a mixture) that leads to a state of arousal. Like men, women's initial spark of desire is based on hormone levels, mood, general health, and attitude about sex. But unlike men, the woman's mounting desire is not based primarily or only on the way her partner looks. Men can very happily view a photograph or other visual image and imagine jack-hammering away, or will put up with a beautiful woman who has a bad personality just to sleep with her. Women, as a rule, require more than visual stimulation to get their motor running. This is not to say women don't have their physical fantasies, especially in modern America where everything is sold with an image of physical perfection—male six packs as well as a woman's "perfect 10" breasts. I've known women who have referred to a man's shoulders "going on for miles" or lustily to his "almighty cock."

Still, when all is said and done, most women require a rap. A scenario. A bonding and setting of mood that goes beyond mere "getting down." And really good-looking men who know they have no rap or are bonding-impaired are usually smart enough to say very little. Why? So the woman herself can supply the emotional components that will take her beyond hormonal desire to the psychological realm of arousal and from there to the physiological. For a woman arousal means that the vagina gets wet with vaginal lubrication and the vagina lengthens. Breasts swell, sometimes become firmer or become supersensitive, and the nipples become erect. Blood rushes to the surface of the skin, and muscles tense. Breathing becomes rapid and shallow. Some women become aroused in virtually the blink of an eye, and orgasm almost immediately. Others take far longer—requiring up to forty-five minutes of foreplay before orgasm is possible. The orgasms of a woman are remarkably similar to those of a man— some women even "ejaculate" vaginal fluid upon climaxing. After the orgasms most women experience a similar loss of sexual and muscular tension as men, their bodies returning to normal. But there is one huge difference: the recovery stage for women is much briefer. In fact some women can have several orgasms in a row.

That's it for our medical, scientific tour of the pleasure zones. From this point forward, the emphasis will be on the good things we can do with these parts. And for that, brothas and sistahs, we need one another.

Mackin'

WHERE AND HOW TO MEET

THE LOVE OF YOUR LIFE

When a boy has thus begun to woo the girl he loves,
he should spend his time with her and amuse her
with various games and diversions fitted for their
age and acquaintanceship.   —*Kama Sutra*

Now that you know how your equipment works, you
probably want to make practical use of your knowledge. Some readers may already be involved in a
committed relationship. In that case, skip to page 55. But for

those still looking for that special someone, the question is, Where can I find her? Where is he at? In my book *Black Pearls Book of Love,* I mention a number of magical practices and charms that are said to switch on your love magnet. If you have an intended and simply want to get his or her attention, then according to one Louisiana folk belief, you should place the person's picture behind a mirror. Another belief from the same area suggests you take some of the desired one's hair and sleep with it under your pillow.

If you don't have a specific person in mind but simply want to create a love vibe and choose from the many people that will be attracted to you, you can follow the following folk recipe from Trinidad: "Boil together marby bark, anise seeds, and nutmeg mace [skin covering the nutmeg shell]. Sweeten with sugar and drink a wineglass of it every day." This concoction is said not only to attract people to you, but because it is reputed to be an aphrodisiac, it will inflame your desire and arousal so that when you make your choice, you will not disappoint him or her.

For those who prefer a more grounded approach to finding a love (or who want to combine charms with a more grounded approach; they are not mutually exclusive), there are many ways to come into contact with the love of your life. One woman gave a party for ten of her single female friends. How is having ten single girlfriends over going to result in a potential male lifemate?

"To get past the doorman, and to step over the threshold of my apartment, each woman had to bring at least one available man," said Tamara, 33, who is a human resources manager for an insurance company in Atlanta. She continued, with a smile: "That way, not only did you have men, but these men had been vetted. They were definitely not scrubs!" Did she find a true love at the end of the evening?

"Well, it was more like at the end of six evenings," said Tamara, who has been in a committed relationship for about a year. "I met him during one of these parties given by one of my friends. And guess what: He is the guy I took as one of the available male singles!"

Tamara's story illustrates the prime directive when it comes to meeting that special someone. In looking for someone to court, or for someone who will court you, only three things matter: numbers, numbers, numbers. Or, as the New York Lotto people say, "You've got to be in it to win it!"

"Before I found my wife, if I had a choice of ways to get somewhere, I would always choose the most populated way," said Bobby, 28, a project manager with a computer company in Palo Alto, California. "If I had to do something and I had my choice of locations—a bank, for instance—I would go to the one I thought would be most crowded. Yes, it took a little longer, but that is how I found my wife. Waiting for a table at a popular restaurant in San Francisco that drew lines for weekend brunch."

There is also the "squeaky wheel gets the grease" technique.

"I just started complaining to my friends," said Lola, a 30-year-old bank secretary. She went on goodnaturedly to say that this is how she met the man who has been in her life for the past three years. "When complaining didn't work, I was more explicit. Periodically, I'd simply ask my friends: 'Do you know of any eligible men?' The problem, of course, is that friends are sometimes reluctant to get involved in another friend's love life. The up side is that the friend has a chance to make two other friends very happy. The down side is that the friend can make two friends very unhappy, if the affair has a crash landing. So I understand the reluctance. Still, if you are looking for someone, at least you should let your friends know. Let them decide whether or not to get involved."

If your friends are hesitant to set you up with a blind date, there is a technological solution: the Internet, which you might augment with a personal ad in an appropriate newspaper or magazine.

"I met my girlfriend on the Internet," said Kirk, 37, an accountant in Minneapolis. "People doubted that I would find someone that way. I talked to my now girlfriend about it after we'd been together awhile, and she too said her friends warned her away from it. But the fact is that you can meet a sociopath anywhere. I have a good female friend who was set up with someone known to a group of her friends. So after their date, when he dropped her off at her apartment, he asked if he could go in and use her bathroom. Ordinarily she wouldn't have let him in, but because he was in her social clique, she said yes. Ten minutes later he emerged from the bathroom wearing only her bathrobe. He soon left without incident, but still, she told me, it was a spooky moment.

Eight steps to a heavenly Internet and periodical personal ad experience . . .

1. Look at existing ads on the site or in the periodical to make sure these are the kind of people you want to be with.

2. Be thoughtful and candid about filling out the questionnaire describing yourself. If you are looking for a relationship that has the possibility of becoming long term, say that in your ad. The people you frighten off are people you wouldn't want to date anyway.

3. Don't be too restrictive when it comes to what you are looking for. If being well-read is most important to you, then include that in the description of the man of your dreams. But try not to give all your wants equal weight. Doing so simply limits the pool of potential candidates and puts you in the position of creating a fantasy mate who doesn't exist in the real world.

4. When replying to an ad, say a few things about why the ad appealed to you. Also give them a brief—two or three sentences—rundown on who you are. (This can be a template paragraph that you send to everyone you respond to.) Finally, in your reply, refer them to your ad, with the invitation to write back if they are intrigued by what they read. The reasons for doing this are: You want to individualize your response so that they know you have really read their ad. Then you want them to know a smidgen about you. Referring them to your ad for a fuller story accomplishes two things: It allows them a longer and more thoughtful look into your personality and interests.

It also makes them invest in you. Someone who doesn't have the energy to click their mouse a couple of times to find out more about you is, again, not someone you want to date anyway.

5. Don't let e-mail correspondences go on too long. An extended e-mail courtship without dating only allows both of you to build unrealistic expectations and fantasies of one another. After a couple of good exchanges, and perhaps a phone call, arrange to meet. Remember, you're looking for a girl- or boyfriend, not a pen pal.

6. When you meet, do it in a public place. Whether you are a man or a woman, this is important for obvious safety reasons.

7. Take the relationship slowly. When all is said and done, you don't know this person from Adam (or Eve). Don't be in a hurry to be alone with them. Don't be in a hurry to give them personal information; allow trust to build. And women, the best way to have a man take his time, not push for sex, and get to know you as a person is to pay for yourself on those initial outings. (Or offer to pay for yourself and *mean it!*)

8. Last, don't restrict your search for a match to those online. It really can atrophy your skills in meeting that someone special in the face-to-face world. So while standing or sitting on a bus, while stopped at a stop light, smile. Flirt. Just let the Internet be an additional arrow in your quiver of ways to find someone.

Keeping an open mind was beside the point in the first-century India of the Kama Sutra, a time and place fraught with social rules to courting: who is appropriate marriage material because of caste, location, and politics. We African Americans in the twenty-first century are far freer. First, we don't have arranged marriages. We can marry whomever we want. Approximately fifty percent of the correspondents said they have or would have a serious relationship with someone of another race. But despite the openness, there were still many reservations.

Would you date out of your race?

I have never dated outside my race. When I was younger, I would never have entertained the thought. Now that I'm older, and I think more open minded, I would probably consider it if I were single. That's a difficult decision because there are so many cultural differences that oftentimes need to be taken into consideration. In fact, the cultural differences within the black race alone (West Indian descendants, Africans, black Hispanics) can be a big mountain to cross.   Julia, 32

There was a time when I would have said, "No way!" But the older I get, the more open I am to the idea. I'm starting to see beauty in people of all races. I once told my oldest son that he had better not ever bring a white girl to sit at my dinner table! But, I had to take that back. I told him to concentrate more on the girl's spirituality instead of her race. I believe those who have a solid relationship with their Maker are able to relate to others more positively.   Bob, 41

As long as I am treated with love and respect. But I would first seek someone from my own race.   Sue, 30

❦❦❦

Until recently I would have to say no. But now I am seriously dating a Native American/Philippino mixed gentleman. In the past I have only dated black men.   June, 39

❦❦❦

I believe if I did, he would be of Hispanic origin because he would be more likely to understand where I'm coming from and how I am trying to get there.   Carolyn, 36

❦❦❦

Probably Hispanic, because I think our cultures are very similar. However, I hope that I'm mature enough to see a person for who they are and not what race they belong to.   Jake, 32

❦❦❦

There wouldn't be a preference—it would have to be the characteristics of a person—their outlook on life and self, the relationship to their friends and family, and their spiritual development. That person would also have to have an appreciation for my culture and heritage—not to adopt it as their own, but they would have to open to discovering the wealth and diversity that I bring to the relationship by virtue of my ethnicity.   Cynthia, 43

"The point is," Kirk continued, "that you can meet weirdos anywhere. Based on my experiences in bars, clubs, and parties, the Internet is as good a place to meet someone as any."

Another way to find someone is simply to live your life. Do the things you enjoy. If you want to go to the zoo, go to the zoo alone or with a friend of the same sex. If you want to learn Chinese (a wise thing to do, since China is the most populated country in the world and presents tremendous commercial possibilities), enroll in a night class in Chinese. Don't go with your mind set on finding someone, but go with the thought that you might *possibly* find someone. Don't be too judgmental about the people you meet. Keep an open mind.

> For those who were open to another race, there was a slight preference for Hispanic, when any preference was expressed.

But dating other black people was still the preference, and as 1990 U.S. census statistics show, the overwhelming majority of black Americans choose to marry other African Americans: 92 percent of black men between 25 and 34 and 96 percent of black women in that age group choose to marry black.

Having said that, are African Americans with lighter skin color and straighter hair more desirable? Once upon a time there was a "paper bag test," whereby a black person could not attend certain African American churches if he or she was darker than a brown paper bag that hung over the church door. Do African Americans subconsciously have a "paper bag test" when it comes to marriage or dating? Judging from our survey respondents, especially among the women, preferences for lighter skin and straighter hair are going the way of the dodo.

When responding to the question of whether hair texture or skin color factored into who they choose to date or marry, the men responded unanimously, mainly using one of two laconic responses—"No." or "Never." Ronald, a 38-year-old auto mechanic living in Miami, explained that he was attracted to darker-skinned women. Another man, a 44-year-old schoolteacher from Oakland, California, said "a deathly pale" black woman would be a turnoff.

The women respondents, typically, were more expansive in their comments, and while some admitted to favoring "lighter-skinned pretty boys," or to "never hav[ing] seriously dated anyone darker than I am," the vast majority used words such as "dark chocolate," "dark mocha," "a dark brown man with curly hair," when color was a factor in describing a physical aspect of their ideal man.

I don't care about how dark he is. I accept the diversity within my race. Connie, 39

∞∞

Being that I'm light, I prefer someone darker than I am.   Gale, 41

∞∞

Color or hair texture is not a factor, I just don't like extremely pink lips. I know that it is silly, and it wouldn't be a determining factor in my search for Mr. Right. But still . . .   Winnie, 26

∞∞

I have a bias toward darker-skinned brothers. Perhaps because I'm dark, I feel more comfortable with brothers that are dark as well.   Mirta, 32

The most controversial issue, if one is to use essays and articles in black magazines as a gauge, the one that has most upset black Americans, is of a black woman making more money than the man. Yet, if our female respondents are to be believed, it is really not much of a problem at all. The man doesn't have to be the CEO of Chrysler or an anchor on a network news show. The men, however, judging from those who answered the survey question, felt a bit conflicted about the prospect of a woman earning more. Howard, a 38-year-old short order cook living in Williamsburg, Virginia, admitted to some discomfort when he dated a lawyer for a couple of years in the late 1990s.

"Hey, I have an ego too," he explained. "It's humbling, but I am a humble man basically."

Frank, 44, a messenger center supervisor from Brooklyn, New York, was less ambivalent. "I'd be proud that she would be interested in me," he said.

According to the women, the man need not make as much as she, but he must have a plan for making his way in the world, and a way of implementing that plan. Here are a few of their comments about dating a man who made significantly less than the man they marry or date.

No, it would not bother me, unless it was thrown in my face and used to put me down.   Yolanda, 22

❦❦❦

If he were hardworking and conservative, no.   Judy, 35

❦❦❦

He has a job. Period. If that job has room for advancement, that is a plus. Nia, 26

❦❦❦

As long as we can pay the bills, I don't care . . . but he must have potential or at least the drive to do something—legal.   Lucille, 30

❦❦❦

As long as he still helps out and if that was the best he could do, I wouldn't mind. I would mind if I knew he could do better, but wouldn't. Nicole, 39

❦❦❦

No, as long as he were comfortable enough with himself and not make it an issue. Money is important, however in a relationship each individual brings many things and there is no written rule that men must be the biggest financial contributor.   Angela, 38

❦❦❦

In the past, not really. But today I prefer a man with more money or prestige. I have kids and don't need a leech. If he doesn't have money, I hope he at least has plans and a record of achieving something in the past. I will then work with him to help if I can. I don't mind helping a friend in this way. Also, if he doesn't have money, then as long as he can sustain himself at the level he is, this is attractive to me. This means that he has focus and is independent.   Karen, 31

I seem attracted to down-to-earth men who are blue collar. I love it. My grandfather was a farmer and I think that if I could find an intellectual in blue jeans overalls or work boots that he would be my ideal man. It takes more than money to make my world go around.   Jacki, 37

And for those women who did date or marry men who made less than they did, there were various consequences, and various ways of handling those consequences, but the overall feeling is that, all things considered, the relationship felt equal and nourishing.

I made more money than my husband. It bothered him, but it didn't bother me, because I felt like we were working together to raise our daughter. Yvonne, 30

My ex-husband made less than I did. I loved him and didn't really care about that aspect. I just adjusted to his contributions to the household to fit his salary level. He was consistent about contributing. As long as the guy can be consistent, it will work out.   Jennifer, 31

I'm in that situation now and am okay with it because he has ambition . . . so long as he keeps striving and doesn't stay in the place he is in for very long, then I'd really care.   Benilda, 26

※

Most of my relationships were with guys who made less money than I did. The relationships ended for various reasons (infidelity, lack of goals, lack of trust, etc.). I don't think any ended because of the money issue, per se.   Felicia, 32

※

I am in a relationship now where he works two full-time jobs. He is taking care of his son, paying for his transportation, and manages for us to enjoy outings together. If he is short, I jump in (has only happened once in our year together) and if I am short, he jumps in.   Donna, 46

※

Yes, I was in a three-year relationship with a man who made less than I did. We took pleasure in simple things. Although I was just starting my career, I made more money and wanted to do things. If he could not afford it, I would surprise him and make it my treat. He did not mind. He always made sure that he surprised me in return, so I never felt like he was taking advantage of me.   Eileen, 36

Money

Is money really the root of all evil? Depends on who is wielding it and for what reason. Is it to indulge, every once in a while, in a treat—a special pair of shoes, a dinner out, a modest but much deserved vacation? Or is it to lord it over the mate? Is it used as a weapon to coerce and manipulate? This applies equally whether it is the man or the woman with the financial upper hand. But since women having the advantage in money matters is generally a more delicate social issue, here are a few pointers—some dos and don'ts for him and her in the event that it is she with the pocket fat with Benjamins.

She should: be supportive in his efforts to better himself; not use her higher income as a weapon during arguments.

He should: have a plan; do the very best to have and keep a legal job; and never, ever ask her for money.

A girl always shows her love by outward signs and actions such as the following: She never looks the man in the face, and becomes abashed when she is looked at by him; under some pretext or other she shows her limbs to him: she looks secretly at him, though he has gone away from her side; hangs down her head when she is asked some question by him, and answers in indistinct words and unfinished sentences, delights to be in his company for a long time, speaks to her attendants in a peculiar tone with the hope of attracting his attention toward her when she is at a distance from him, and does not wish to go from the place where he is; under some pretext or other she makes him look at different things, narrates to him tales and stories very slowly so that she may continue conversing with him for a long time.

—Kama Sutra

Now that we've made an excursion into the land of money—what the women who answered the survey demand from a man financially and in terms of fiscal ambition and responsibility—we push out to sea to explore what they seek in a man emotionally. What they consider his responsibility. Is there a level of emotional ambition they are looking for? Is it true that they are longing for the silent type, a staple of the masculine mythology of yore? Or do they want a "new man" who cries at the drop of a kente cloth?

Emotionally speaking, what do black women want?

I'm pretty emotional, so my partner must be able to hang with me and be aware of his own feelings and be able and willing to share them. Affection and a loving nature is good. But I think self-knowing is real important. Many folks walk through life in emotional denial and don't even know what's really driving them.   Rita, 48

666

Someone who is open to compromise, self-development, and support. I think that if you are open to change, and willing to meet someone halfway, you have a foundation for an excellent relationship. Not only are you part of the process, but you help encourage as well. Heather, 26

666

It's important to have someone who is able to be honest with themselves, and me as well. Having the ability and courage to express themselves is very important.   Helen, 38

666

He can show emotion and express his feelings to me.   Rhoda, 42

☾☾☾

A strong sense of self and being able to tell me when something is bothering him.   Paula, 26

☾☾☾

A man who is in touch with his emotional side is important. (Can you cry in front of me, are you aware of how you feel about the important people in your life?) I know so many men who are emotionally crippled—for whatever reason they can't handle anything that involves emotional turmoil like being in love, so they shy away from it.   Elizabeth, 26

☾☾☾

That he has emotions, not too soft. Firm. Can take control when he needs to be a man and gentle enough to know when to just let things be!   Frances, 30

But what about men? What do they want from their woman? Passivity? A sepia-tinted Barbie doll, or a strong woman who is capable of being an equal partner in their relationship? Do the men confirm the worst stereotypes of the hard rock who is insensitive, inattentive, and driven entirely by testosterone? Or do they have a tender underbelly that they would only expose to a woman they can trust—the woman of their dreams? Turns out that the men in the survey, while less voluble than women on the subject, are looking for similar things in a woman that the women are looking for in a man. And the constant refrain for the men was the desire and need for something more than arm candy or a momentary release of tension from a woman to whom they would make a major commitment.

Just Say Hello

Some of us are blessed when it comes to meeting members of the opposite sex. They are silver throated and can say no wrong. That, however, is the minority. But take heart. It is not necessary to be a verbal Svengali. The best pickup line, or approach, whether it is man to woman or woman to man, seems to be the simplest: "Hello, my name is . . . ," sometimes with a flourish of "What's your name?" or "And I think you are beautiful." Of course, there are some people who seem not to need even that. "My job speaks for me; ladies like the brown uniform," said Justin, a 31-year-old driver and deliveryman for UPS. But those of us who don't work for UPS, and who don't resemble Tyson or Denzel Washington, can still find the mate of our dreams. Here are the responses to "What was the best pickup line or approach you've ever used or had used on you?" "Just being myself and letting the woman know that I'm interested in her," said Abraham, 33, an insurance salesman in Denver. Recalling a recent approach, Eileen, a 36-year-old elementary school teacher in St. Paul, Minnesota, said, "The gentleman simply walked over and introduced himself and asked if he could sit and talk to me."

"I just love it when a man is old fashioned enough and up front enough to walk up to me and properly introduce himself and ask me my name and then compliment me with something like 'You're so beautiful, I just had to come here and speak to you,'" said Eva, 41, a registered nurse in Hartford, Connecticut.

> **Top ten list of what black women crave emotionally from their man.**
>
> Respect
> Honesty
> Self-confidence
> Fun
> Emotional availability
> Intelligence
> Compassion and passion
> Wisdom
> Affection
> Spirit

All this gives the impression that it is the men who choose the women. Many would argue that it is the other way around—that the woman is the hunter, and that she lures the men she fancies into her lair.

One woman said she and her girlfriends prided themselves on simply planting themselves near the man whose attention they desired. This worked for her without fail—until it came to meeting the man of her dreams.

"I did the usual," said Dolores, a 28-year-old attorney from Riverside, California. "I saw this fine brother at a Halloween party, so I inconspicuously made my way over to where he was standing. I stood there for five minutes. Nothing! Cleared my throat, dropped my lipstick on purpose. No reaction. Other guys started talking to me, and I had to get rid of them without appearing to be unavailable to the guy I was interested in. Finally, I decided I was going to have to break the ice. He was dressed all in black, so I asked if he was costumed as the night. He said no, he had taken off his costume because it was too hot in the apartment. He had come as a ghost."

After a few minutes of conversation, the two girlfriends Dolores had come with said they wanted to leave.

"I dropped all kinds of hints that I would be leaving, still he didn't ask for my number," Dolores recalled. "Finally, I figured he simply wasn't interested in me, so I left. As I was entering the elevator, he ran and got on the elevator with me. On the way down, he asked me for my number."

What happened in the interim with the man?

"My best friend whispered to me that if I didn't get her number, I was nuts," said Jovan, 32, a computer graphics designer from Oakland, who was visiting friends in the Los Angeles area.

And why hadn't he responded to Dolores's charms before?

"Well, I was late to the party, it was hot, and I had had to improvise a costume, so at first I simply didn't notice," he said. "And when I noticed she was flirting, I don't know. I just froze up. Can't explain it."

The couple went on to get married two years after meeting, but Dolores said it was a lesson she would never forget, and one that she passes on to friends.

"Sometimes you have to be the aggressor," she said. "And you have to be 'obvious,' even if you risk rejection." She added with a laugh, "Now I know what men go through all the time."

Despite Dolores's revelation, men and women seem to be equally divided as to whether it is appropriate for a woman to be the aggressor in the very obvious "let's get this conversation started" kind of way. Some are loathe to do it, feeling that it is either "unladylike" or is an indication of desperation. Some women even see having to talk first to a man as a blow to their egos, an indication that they are not very attractive. "I don't *need* to go up to men," said a 22-year-old waitress from Las Vegas. "They *always* come to me."

Other women will approach a man at the drop of a hat, with no threat to their egos and no concern about the man's ultimate reaction.

"Frankly, if a man gets spooked by me showing interest in him, that is not the kind of man I want anyway," said Jill, 37, an interior designer from White Plains, New York. "It's good that I know from the get-go. Besides, I'm not trying to sleep with a guy I approach at a party. I think he is attractive in some way, and I'm just trying to get to know him. That is the vibe I am trying to project—friendly curiosity."

Some men find a woman's aggression a turn-on and react positively to it. Others find it a turn-on but react negatively to it.

"I'm not a bad-looking guy," said one man from Austin. "I get a fair number of women who smile at me throughout the day, and I enjoy the attention. It's an ego boost. But after the smile, I'd prefer to be in charge. I just feel it's the man's role."

> When a girl . . . wishes to bring about her own marriage when she comes of age, such a girl . . . should try to get alone with her beloved in some quiet place, and at odd times should give him flowers, betel nut, betel leaves, and perfumes. . . . She should also talk to him on subjects he likes best.
>
> — Kama Sutra

If the man is going to initiate things, as was stated earlier, a simple "hello" is usually good enough. But sometimes it takes men a long time to learn that simple lesson.

"I was faithful during my marriage, and didn't even really flirt," said Stanley, 40, a divorced buyer for a department store in Cleveland. "So when I first began approaching women, it was 'Hummena, hummena, hummena.' As you can imagine, that lack of self-assurance really turned them off. Then one day, my kids and I were watching *The Mighty Ducks,* a Disney film about a children's hockey team. During one scene, the team was trying to get the goalie to overcome her fear of the hockey puck flying at her. So they tied her to the goal posts and shot pucks at her. In her uniform, mask, and padding, of course. That way, they showed her that (a) she could take the pain of getting hit with a puck and (b) that it didn't hurt that much anyway.

"A lightbulb went off in my head: What I needed to do in terms of dating was think of an analogous situation. I pondered the question for a few days and remembered a comment I overheard two female colleagues in my office make many years ago. One had mentioned to the other that she thought Spike Lee was cute, then caught herself. 'Oh that's right,' the woman said to the other, 'you don't like short men.'

"At five-eight, I never considered myself short—maybe the shorter side of average, but I certainly had no complexes about my height. I was steadily dating my wife-to-be by then, so the impact of the statement was minimal. I was not looking for anyone else. But once I was back on the dating scene, however, it was devastating to my self-confidence.

> But when the man shows his wish to enjoy her, she should be favorable to him, and all the manifestations of his love, as if she were ignorant of the state of his mind. But when he tries to kiss her she should oppose him; when he begs to be allowed to have sexual intercourse with her she should let him touch her private parts only and with considerable difficulty.
>
> —Kama Sutra

After watching the videotape of the movie, *The Mighty Ducks,* I had an idea: I'd walk up to tall women—women more or less my height, or a couple of inches taller—and just say hello. I'd have no agenda other than saying hello and keeping the conversation going for a couple of minutes. Since I was expecting rejection, I figured that it would be the equivalent of a hockey puck hurtling toward me. A way of learning that I could live through the rejection so that I could eventually approach women I was really interested in.

"My plan worked—except for one thing: I found that I was not rejected nearly as much as I thought I would be. Certainly no more than by women under five-eight. So my exercise ended up giving me a whole new pool of women to approach. And as we all know, trying to find Ms. Right is a numbers game, anyway."

But some men complain that even after having made their approach, they don't get clear signals from a woman on whether they have lit her fire.

"Often, I'll talk to a woman for half an hour, only to find out she has, or says she has, a boyfriend," said Brian, 33, an investment researcher who lives in Queens, New York. "And frequently they don't tell me on purpose, which means I have effectively just wasted my time. Either I am told by a friend or they tell me by mistake."

Avery, a 35-year-old television news producer in Miami, noticed the same trend and devised a formula to cull those women simply ego-tripping on his attentions from those who are really interested in him.

"When I see a woman I like, I am very direct," he said. "First, I compliment her in some way so that she knows my interest is not Platonic. Then I ask if she has a boyfriend, husband, or significant other. I don't always ask the question directly, but I might say something like 'You have lovely eyes. Your boyfriend is a lucky guy to wake up to those eyes every morning'—or something like that. If she tells me she is unattached, then I ask what kind of men she likes. I'm a little overweight, so if a woman says she likes outdoorsy kinds of guys or 'athletic' guys, I can assume she wouldn't be interested in me, and I am out of there. I ask those questions within the first three minutes with a woman.

"I know some guys feel that they can 'work' a woman and make her come around to being interested in them," Avery continued. "I have no doubt that that can happen and have seen it on many occasions. But I prefer the path of least resistance. I figure why try to turn around a woman when I can spend an equal amount of energy, or less, looking for a woman who is interested in me and will meet me half-way. Seems like a more efficient use of my time."

While "Hello, I'm . . ." seems to be the hands-down favorite, here are some fun approaches that our correspondents said are unlikely to offend:

These lines got game

"I like what I see, but I would like to get to know the beauty you have inside."   Tina, 33.

⊙⊙⊙

I have no idea what he said, but it was nice to hear it in French. Aisha, 26

⊙⊙⊙

"You sure have pretty hair."   Elizabeth, 24

⊙⊙⊙

My mate of four years told me that we had a vibe—it actually ended up being true because we still have it.   Benilda, 26

⊙⊙⊙

"Hi, how have you been? I haven't seen you in such a long time." (And that was followed by a hug!) He really had me going for a minute like I really knew him.   Sue, 30

⊙⊙⊙

"When I first laid eyes on you I knew God sent you to me."   Peg, 43

⊙⊙⊙

"Is your husband married?"   Marie, 39

These lines are lame

"Is your husband married?"   Georgia, 30

666

He said to me, "Baby you look so good, I could sop you up with a biscuit." How disgusting!   Bernice, 36

666

One time I walked into a music store and this guy stares at my chest and starts guessing my breast size! Just throwin' sizes out like 36C, 38C . . . Jamilah, 21

666

"I seem to have lost my phone number, can I borrow yours?"   Kimberly, 30

666

"Hey, Momma, want to get with me?"   Alexandra, 44

666

This guy walked up to me and said, "Damn, you got some big titties." Beverly, 18

666

"When was the last time anyone ravished your voluptuous body?" Leontine, 30

666

"With all this heat, Chocolate, you might melt in the sun."   Ada, 29

666

"What's your sign?" My response, "No trespassing."   Louise, 34

"Yo, Momma, are you waiting for me?"   Iris, 40

※

He said to me, "I would enjoy licking you like a lollipop and when I reached the center, I would eat you up!" And then a loud slurping sound.   Aminah, 29

※

"I would love to be looking at your beautiful face across the breakfast table in the morning."   Mattie, 25

※

"Do I know you?"   Elsie, 39

※

"That dress looks good on you, but it would look better on my floor." Sandi, 16

※

"You must be tired, because you have been running through my mind all day."   Jill, 26

※

"You have been classified as a Tenderoni."   Hope, 32

Folk sayings, regardless of the topic, give guidance and serve as a repository of age-old wisdom. The most current example is "It takes a village to raise a child," an African saying that has gained currency in mainstream America. The truth of the statement is obvious: every child requires more than any one person can give. There are many reasons for this. First, the child simply might be more temperamentally attuned to someone else in the community, or that person may share more of the child's interests. Also, parents cannot be everywhere at once. Children, as they should, go off on their own to play games, explore their envi-

50

ronment, and begin creating their own minisocieties with their peers. Yet, they still require supervision, and the thousand eyes of the community monitoring the child, making sure he or she is not forming bad habits, is in the best interest of the child, the parents, and the society at large. The thousand embracing arms of the community make sure the child is safe, make sure that he or she is challenged but not overwhelmed.

There are, of course, tens of thousands of folk sayings. The African proverb "God gives nothing to those who keep their arms crossed" reminds us that good things happen to those who anticipate them and are prepared to grab opportunity when it arises. "You shake man han', you no shake him heart" is the Jamaican version of "Everyone who smiles in your face is not your friend," and an important admonition not to be naive about other people's motives. The Kenyan proverb "On the way to one's beloved there are no hills" reminds us that when we are full of a sense of purpose, it seems as if there are no obstacles between us and our goal, regardless of what it is. Our desire turns mountains into plains, tortuous winding roads into straightaways.

Our ancestors and our ancestors' ancestors have said much about love over the millennia. If it were put down on paper, it would fill up volumes. Below is a smattering of the folk wisdom from black communities that have given comfort, helped maintain faith, and guided black people for years and years and years in the creation of strong, nurturing romantic unions.

Look at how he treats his momma, and that is how he will treat you.

The blacker the berry, the sweeter the juice.

Just be patient. God will send you your mate, but only when you are right with God, and true to yourself.

Don't go looking for love. When it's your time, love and the right person will find you.

You must be equally yoked.

When people show you who they are the first time, believe them.

Let go and let God.

Make a list of what you want from a man in a relationship and stick with that list.

Listen to your heart and go with what feels right.

Don't get your honey where you get your money.

Find one just like your daddy.

Love yourself and be comfortable with yourself. Be a complete individual.

Never judge a book by its cover.

You won't meet a husband on the dance floor.

When her love begins to show signs of increasing, he should relate to her agreeable stories, if she expresses a wish to hear such narratives. Or if she takes delight in legerdemain, he should amaze her by performing various tricks of jugglery; or if she feels a great curiosity to see a performance of the various arts, he should show his own skill in them. When she is delighted with singing, he should entertain her with music, and on certain days, and at the time of going together to moonlight fairs and festivals, and at the time of her return after being absent from home, he should present her with bouquets of flowers and with chaplets for the head and with ear ornaments and rings, for these are the proper occasions on which such things should be presented.

—Kama Sutra

In the Realm of the Senses

WHAT TO WEAR, WHAT TO EAT, SMELLIN' GOOD

As most of us know, sex is not just a matter of inter-locking parts, like a Lego set or a Lincoln Logs cabin plaything. It involves the use of all of our senses—sight, taste, touch, smell, even hearing—to an unprecedented degree. Sex is probably the most potent physical experience we will ever voluntarily undergo. It's bungee jumping, a day at the race track, running a marathon, eating the tastiest peach, all rolled into one. The acrid odor of unwashed armpits, the scent of a light perfume, the scratchiness of ungroomed toenails, the feathery touch of a lotioned palm sliding over smooth skin, can unleash the tiger in us or make as want to scurry like a bunny in the face of a close encounter of the sexual kind.

Personal grooming also helps us feel confident about ourselves and, in making us feel confident about ourselves, helps us relax so that we are open to receiving the attentions of others. I once took a quick trip to the grocery store with a platonic female friend of mine. Before leaving her apartment she changed clothes, put on lipstick, and I think she even dabbed on a spot of perfume. When I reminded her that we were just stepping out for a couple of sandwiches and would be coming right back to eat them, she said, "You never know who you are going to meet," and recounted how she'd once taken a "quick trip" for breakfast items.

Waiting to buy her items, she noticed a very cute man two lines away. His mocha-colored face was framed by a lion's mane of dreads. His warm, megawatt smile beamed in her direction. He looked intelligent and artistic; confident, but not cocky. On the face of it, just her type. But she never had a chance to find out. She wanted to reciprocate the smile, but looked away instead. Once she bought her items, she looked up and was surprised to see the same heart-melting smile. He extended his hand. "Hello," he said, "I'm Charles." But while she shook his hand, she felt so ratty that during the ensuing minute-long conversation she never looked up at him or returned his smile. She felt so uncomfortable with her morning breath that she stayed a distance from him, and that communicated distrust or get lost. And so after a minute or two of trying to engage her, he left.

"It's not that this man was the love of my life," my friend said. "But who knows, he might have been. The important thing I learned was that I'll never know, all because I didn't take a couple of minutes to get myself together."

"It's not like I want him to be pedicured," another friend said about a man she met who had unkempt feet. "I like the hardness of a man, a bit of rough-

In the pleasure room, decorated with flowers, and fragrant with perfumes, attended by his friends and servants, the citizen should receive the woman, who will come bathed and dressed, and will invite her to take refreshment and to drink freely. . . . They should then carry on an amusing conversation on various subjects, and may also talk suggestively of things which would be considered as coarse, or not to be mentioned generally in society. They may then sing, either with or without gesticulations, and play on musical instruments, talk about the arts, and persuade each other to drink. At last, when the woman is overcome with love and desire, the citizen should dismiss the people that may be with him. . . . Such is the beginning of sexual union.

—Kama Sutra

ness. But I do wish that he'd take just ten or fifteen minutes every week to use pumice on the calluses on his heels. That roughness just feels nasty rubbing up against my skin."

But even before an expectation of sexual contact, there is the sensuality of creating or finding the right atmosphere—low lights, the voice of Marvin Gaye or Al Green wafting through the room, the right food, the right clothes, scented candles, perhaps. This section is dedicated to setting the stage for loving.

Most of the time foul odors from the underarm, pubic area, or mouth are the result of lack of attention or lack of common sense. Regardless of how the situation came about, what they communicate is lack of respect for your partner—not the message you want to project to the one you may potentially love. Short of needing medical attention, most distasteful odors—halitosis, foul body odor—are easily dealt with.

Don't try to cover up. A breath mint or gum to cover up bad breath will probably end up making matters worse—the scent of the breath freshener will only very temporarily mask bad breath, and shortly after the bad breath will return coupled with the artificial smell of the gum or mint. Ugh! Get biannual dental cleanings. Brush regularly AND floss. Also, try brushing the back of your tongue with your toothbrush. (You can also buy a tongue scraper.) If you are out and had shrimp scampi with a little too much garlic, try munching on a sprig or two of parsley (just be sure you're able to check for bits of the green stuff stuck between your teeth) or Breath Assure or some such product, which doesn't cover your breath, but neutralizes bad odors. If your halitosis persists beyond these simple remedies, you should see your doctor.

With foul body odor (not all body odor is unattractive, after all), the same thing goes. Don't try to cover up, just wash with soap and water. And then perhaps a little deodorant. Again, don't cover up with perfumes or colognes. Their scents won't eliminate your funk, only mingle with it, making you a walking perfumed garbage heap. One of the biggest complaints from the respondents was that their partner—overwhelmingly the male—didn't wash after exercising or after a night of dancing at a club, and then wants to "get down" immediately upon returning to the apartment. "I met this truly gorgeous man. We talked several times, and then decided to meet for the real deal. Well, I got to his house, and he was smelling. He said that he had been working out."

"There is no reason for a person to have body odor unless he cannot smell," said Ada, 29, a parole officer who lives in Boston. "I dated a person who jogged and would sit on the couch after jogging, all sweaty and musty. Additionally, he took garlic pills and other health-food supplements that came out in his skin. To say the least, his lack of attention to his hygiene after jogging did not hinder me from deciding to break it off with him."

"I had a sexual relationship with this guy who didn't seem to care about how he smelled when he crawled into bed," said Cindy, a 30-year-old secretary from San Diego, California. "Don't get me wrong. He showered in the morning, but I think that may have been it. He would be out all day and then would go to the club, then come to my house after that, feet and armpits kicking. BAD. I love a man that always smells good, even if it is just soap and water. That would be fine."

Some would say that soap and water might be the extent of what one should do. In 1974 researchers at Emory University in Atlanta isolated what they called "sex attractant" secretions called pheromones in women's vaginas. Later, scientists discovered evidence of similar "sex attractant" secretions in men's underarms. The degree to which those smells act as babe and stud magnets on humans is debatable, though they are a proven aphrodisiac in monkeys, mice, moths, and even species that don't begin with *m*'s, such as pigs. Scientists have long known that in the animal kingdom, most species identify potential mates through their highly developed sense of smell, and some research has indicated that humans may possess a similar kind of sensitivity. While the evidence is far from conclusive, one researcher believes that humans may fall in love at first smell rather than first sight.

In the mid 1990s the cosmetic and perfume industry took advantage of this possibility and initiated a fad by creating colognes and perfumes with synthetically produced human pheromones, the idea being that one whiff and the opposite gender would be ineluctably drawn to the wearer. The result was decidedly mixed. What seemed incontrovertible, however, was that people who dabbed these science-lab pheromones on their pulse points *felt* better about themselves, and exuded, if not sexuality, at least confidence, and that that in itself had a beneficial effect on attracting members of the opposite sex.

But we are not rutting pigs, and it's doubtful that the funk resulting from a five-mile run ever acted as an aphrodisiac, even for our Cro-Magnon forebears. On the other hand, we often talk about "chemistry" in a relationship, so maybe there's something to all of this talk of pheromones.

Take a hint from Lynn, a 30-year-old lawyer from New Orleans, who wrote: "Although I think the musky scent of a man is very sexy, when it gets to be overpowering, then I must object. But you can make grooming a very sensuous experience. For instance, having my man sit between my legs while I massage and oil his scalp is one of the best forms of foreplay around."

> He should wear a fine dress, and make as good an appearance as possible, for young women love men who live with them, and who are handsome, good looking, and well dressed.
>
> — Kama Sutra

Amen to that. And it could save a relationship. If simple soap and water don't eliminate bad body odor, check out your diet or lifestyle. For instance, eating lots of garlic or even swallowing garlic pills may seep through the skin, giving off an unpleasant odor. And everyone knows smoking permeates the skin, making clothes, furniture, and bed linen smell like an ashtray full of ashes from cheap cigarettes.

Clothes are more important than most of us would care to acknowledge. We want to think that we are beyond that kind of thinking, that we are too deep. We want to believe that we look at the inner person and base our opinions on that, not the clothes a person wears. Still, there is a saying in the business world that clothes do indeed make the man—or woman. If that is not true, then thousands of pages have been wasted giving guidance on dressing for success—red power ties versus yellow power ties; whether the hem of the dress should hit the knee or below the knee; the importance of buffing your oxfords or wingtips to such a high gloss that you can shave in their reflection.

It should come as no surprise, then, that work is not the only arena in which clothes make an important impression. It should also come as no surprise that work is not the only arena where you dress for where you want to be, not for where you are. In the game of love, attire is important. Clothes are a kind of uniform, or more accurately, a kind of pheromone, whose purpose is to get the partner into the mood.

For our correspondents black was not only beautiful, it was the sexiest color. When dressing with a tryst in mind, the color most likely to conjure body heat was black. Red was a distant second. The cliché that women are more turned on by what is going on inside a man, and men more interested in the outer woman, seemed to hold true in this part of the survey. Men were fairly unanimous in what they thought was sexy on a woman—something form fitting and discreetly revealing.

"I like to see my girlfriend in a short black tight number, with nothing on underneath," said Earl, 26, a computer programmer living in San Francisco. "Drives me wild." Alan, 27, a high school math teacher from Nashville, Tennessee, said he likes to see his wife in a "short strapless red or black dress with really high heels (and no panty hose)." At clubs, Matt, 22, a graduate student in Cambridge, Massachusetts, said the women who get his attention first are the ones dressed in "a black leather pants suit with a halter top, or dressed in the halter top with a black leather miniskirt. And the women should be wearing four-inch-high black leather pumps."

Women seem to be comfortable with this ideal of sexiness, and frequently said they themselves feel super appealing when wearing leather, Lycra, halter tops, and steep pumps when they want to feel special with that special man.

"To feel sexy I like to wear something that is short, but still long enough that I can sit down comfortably," said Iris, 21, a student from Columbus, Ohio. "I top it off with something red or black that is form fitting. Or I might wear a sleeveless dress with heels."

For more intimate occasions the sky is the limit. "Before my sweetie passed

What men want

"Emotional stability and consistency are the most important things for me when it comes to a prospective girlfriend or wife." Brad, 30

⊙⊙⊙

"I can sum it up in one word: *affection.*" Jon, 44

⊙⊙⊙

"I am looking for a sincere expression of their emotions." Jake, 38

⊙⊙⊙

"A sense of humor is very important, as is emotional security and intelligence." Kwame, 25

⊙⊙⊙

"Self-confidence." Todd, 44

---

away, I would wear this black nasty lingerie outfit for him. It had a tight black lace corset and black crotchless panties with thigh-high stockings. . . . Boy I was fierce in that outfit, you hear me!?" said Kira, 46, a real estate agent in Washington, D.C.

Beth, a 26-year-old housewife in Newark, New Jersey, feels most sexy in a dress of hers that leaves little to the imagination. "I have this black dress that really fits that is completely see through except in a few discreet places," she said.

While men and women seem to basically agree on what makes a woman look sexy, what makes a man look sexy is a little more up for grabs. Both men and women liked the way men looked in a tuxedo or a tailored suit. Philip, 30, a personnel manager in New York City, said he felt sexy in "a nice three-piece suit with a pocket watch. Spit-shined shoes, and a gold hoop earring," and many of the other men said they felt sexy in a suit. Lynette, 31, a college professor in Chicago, might have an explanation for why suits and tuxedos are so appealing to both men and women. "Men seem to have an air of power in a suit or a tuxedo," she said, echoing the sentiments of many of the women correspondents. "Those clothes really turn me on." Bessie, 31, said that she likes it when her man spices up the usual Armani or Ralph Lauren duds. "My ex-husband, who is Latin, used to take me to sexy salsa occasions, where he would dress in colorful suits and beautiful matching ties."

But power, the women said, is not only projected through a suit. A man's body, tastefully revealed, is another turn-on, as is a strong sense of cultural pride. "Nothing is more sexy than to see a brother decked out in African garb," said Felicia, 32, a radio producer in Charleston, South Carolina. "Brothers are gorgeous in cloth from the motherland." Marianne of Jackson, Mississippi, said, "I like the clothes worn by men in martial arts movies. They look so masculine, noble, and exotic with their soft, natural fabric with an Asian or African flair."

According to their responses women like a slice of beefcake the way men enjoy cheesecake, and that also affects how the women like to see men dressed. "I like men with big arms and chest, so anything that will show off those assets is fine," said Gwen, 28, a beautician living in Detroit. "I saw a man that wore a nice fitted sweater and a pair of dress pants. He looked very nice."

Evelyn of Chicago seconded Gwen's opinion. "In public, a nice silk shirt, unbuttoned halfway down. Nice fitting—not male prostitute tight, but tight enough that I can see his goodies," the 30-year-old anthropology professor, said. "In the bedroom I want him in silk boxers."

In fact men's legs, as shown off in bikini underwear, boxers, or shorts, were very popular. "I like to see men in shorts," said Sherry, 36, a dental assistant in Seattle. "But most men do not wear them for fear of the way their legs look."

So now you've met, whether at a party or online, and had your first in-person chat, say while in line for a popular movie. You've gone out a couple of times.

Physical traits women want in their man

Most important: eyes and his smile.   Faith, 36

🌀🌀🌀

Cute lips and eyes and taller than me.   Gail, 31

🌀🌀🌀

Sexy smooth skin, muscular arms and legs, clean appearance (trimmed facial hair, if any). A sense of style is very attractive, and a beautiful smile.   Carolee, 21

🌀🌀🌀

Big, muscular, dark skinned.   Corinne, 30

🌀🌀🌀

Strong looking. Not skinny, but very masculine looking.   Adrianne, 28

🌀🌀🌀

I like them dark, with long lashes!   Eva, 41

🌀🌀🌀

Being well groomed.   Alyse, 45

🌀🌀🌀

Height, grooming, a little weight does not matter. Obesity would. Maria, 39

You look good and the person you are looking at looks good. You smile easily, maintain eye contact. You feel comfortable, and the genie of chemistry has been unleashed. Your heart is pumping and you're feeling tingly all over, perhaps even a little lightheaded. You are alone with that special someone, and want to take the relationship to the next level. We're entering into the realm of foreplay.

Once, while trying to gain some insight into the female sexual psyche, I asked a lesbian friend about women and foreplay. Should one start at the toes and work up? Or start at the forehead and work down? Are the breasts really that important? In terms of manipulating the clitoris, can there be too much of a good thing? Should foreplay last fifteen minutes? A half an hour? At what part of the date should foreplay begin?

My friend peered at me over her rose-colored granny glasses, and gave my ignorance a look that seemed equal parts pity and humor. After a pause she said, "Honey, it's all foreplay."

I was a young man at the time, and learned through subsequent conversations with her and other female friends that foreplay lasts not only through the length of a candlelit dinner. It is not just the come-hither looks and suggestive smiles following a glass of red wine or one of those sugary drinks with the little paper umbrellas in them. Foreplay is a lifestyle, at least for couples who have the most successful romantic relationships. Foreplay does not necessarily lead to sex, let alone orgasm, although it by no means veers away from it.

The foreplay of most couples I spoke to who live their sexual lives with passion consisted of a steady affirmation of their mate's attractiveness and value as a human being. It can arrive any time of the day or night. It can be as suggestive as secreting a pair of panties in a briefcase for an office forget-me-not (just make sure you are not going to surprise him during a major presentation in front of clients!), or as tender as a light touch on the knee on the way to the mall to run routine errands. What is foreplay, and what is its purpose? I put that question to the correspondents.

Foreplay is . . .

The fuse for the bomb that you are trying to set off.   Gabriel, 30

666

Can begin with a poem, a kiss, a call in the middle of the day, and a sharing of fantasies. Two people have very different rhythms, and foreplay helps them to become one. This is the reason why foreplay is so important, but so very few people understand its necessity or tap into its power.   Lance, 30

666

Isn't always kissing and touching. It could consist of only conversation. Cara, 26

666

Is conversation, touching, kissing, petting, and it is supposed to get both parties relaxed and in the mood to share with each other sexually. Ella, 27

666

Is appreciating, friendly, warm, cooperative . . . different astrological signs like different techniques. Example: Leos like to be kissed and stroked or lightly blown on their back.   Justine, 32

666

Is everything from kissing to touching to taking each other's clothes off to caressing and kissing various parts of the body. It is to build a momentum toward the sexual encounter.   Iman, 37

666

Allows you to remember only the passion at hand.   Laurel, 29

666

Starts waaaaay before we get to the bedroom (or wherever it takes place). It involves exploring each other's body, developing a rhythm for what is to come. It's supposed to make each of us hunger for the main course.   Kendra, 44

666

Is setting the mood. It can be with sweet talk, music, candles, massage, caress, or anything that stimulates you and your partner.   Amy, 42

666

Is to get one to a plateau of arousal to have a fantastic orgasm, the release of pent-up arousal.   Calvin, 25

666

Is kissing, touching, massaging, looking, hugging, laughing.   Alicia, 33

Thinking Outside the Box

Too often, what we consider the sexy parts of a human being, those parts that are supposed to be the supreme conduit for chills and thrills to the body and the mind, the ones we usually focus on during sex, are painfully and pitifully restricted. Seldom do people look beyond the usual suspects—the lips, the breasts and nipples (men usually don't even get that stimulation), perhaps the ears, and, of course, the genitals, for sensual pleasure. But the body is a symphony orchestra. In the course of most sexual encounters this orchestra is seldom played to its fullest. Whole sections—the strings, the woodwinds, for instance—wait patiently for the conductor to point his baton in their direction. But instead he keeps it trained on the booming tympany and blaring brass. And they are directed to play forte!

Skillful lovers know how to integrate subtler instruments of the body into their sexual compositions. They know one grows tired of listening to a constant booming and blaring. A purr here and there is welcome. Variation is the spice.

When engaged with her in any game or sport, he should intentionally hold her hand. He should practice upon her the various kinds of embraces, such as the touching embrace. . . . He should show her a pair of human beings cut out of the leaf of a tree, and such like things, at intervals. When engaged in water sports, he should dive at a distance from her, and come up close to her. . . . At parties and assemblies of his caste he should sit near her, and touch her under some pretense or other, and having placed his foot upon hers, he should slowly touch each of her toes, and press the ends of the nails; if successful in this, he should get hold of her foot with his hand and repeat the same things. . . . Whenever he gives anything to her or takes anything from her, he should show her by his manner and looks how much he loves her.

—Kama Sutra

Even before stripping down and getting down, the skillful lover thinks about unorthodox ways to deliver sexual pleasure, and creative ways of stimulating it.

"I was in a café with this guy, when we got our hot chocolates," said Ayla, a 24-year-old landscaper from Detroit. "He didn't drink his for a long while. Finally, he gently took my index finger, dipped it in his chocolate like a swizzle stick, and slowly licked it off. It was astonishing. I get shivers just thinking about it."

Another display in the corner of a restaurant occurred to Crystal, a 21-year-old accounting student who lives in Baton Rouge, Louisiana.

"During dessert this man I was out with gently took hold of my hand and started just sort of caressing my palm with his thumb," Crystal remembers. "He then let go and started opening packages of sugar, all the while continuing the casual conversation we were having, as if nothing unusual were happening. I couldn't figure out what he was up to. He started to pour the sugar, so that it outlined a heart, into my open palm. He told me that the symbol for 'heart' really had nothing to do with the muscle in our chest, but was a stylized version of the female sexual organ. Then he slowly and deliciously started licking the sugar from my hand. I have to tell you, I almost had an orgasm right there in the restaurant!"

Fingers and hands: As you may have gathered from the comments of Crystal and Ayla, hands provide an ideal erotic zone. The reasons: They are the most accessible, and are perfect for surprise erotic attacks. Yet, they are discreet: you can give a quick nibble to the fleshy part of the hand before getting in line for a movie, and nobody would be the wiser. The hands are also a conduit for feelings of both affection and lust. Don't just focus on the fingers. Play with the whole hand. Rub your fingers lightly over the top of your partner's hand so that you barely touch the hairs; gently nibble your partner's palm, or sandwich your partner's hand between your hands and delicately knead their hand or intertwine your fingers with theirs. Keep working it and use your imagination.

Face, neck, and shoulders: Like the hands, the face and neck are fairly easy to get at, the shoulders slightly less so. But unlike the hands it is difficult to get

at them without the whole world seeing you. So, unless you are feeling especially exhibitionistic or demonstrative, it is probably best to explore those areas at home. But there you will find a rich field. One game you can play is to refrain from using your mouth on the face, neck, and shoulders. Try using only your hands, and do it lightly and slowly. Try to find erogenous zones in those areas that even your partner didn't know existed. Then try the same with your face, but don't use your lips. Use your forehead, cheeks, closed eyelids, and explore your partner's body with them, making your way down the shoulders and across the back.

Torso: To explore this erogenous zone you'd ideally be at home, or someplace where you are comfortable and in private. Although, come to think of it, a hand around the waist, even if that waist is protected by a shirt or blouse, can be sensual with the right rub or hug. The torso, and especially the sides, can send shivers down the spine with the right touch. As with most sensual approaches a light contact, with an occasional firm press, works wonders. Experiment!

The feet: You've heard of the agony of de feet. I'm going to tell you about the ecstasy of de feet. As with the hands, thousands of nerves end in the feet, and they are sensitive. People who specialize in acupressure say that another advantage to the bundle of nerves ending in the feet is that they serve as a channel to other organs in the body. Regardless, a little fancy footwork can open the door to all sorts of unexpected sensual pleasures, especially if you try massaging them with oil. (Be sure to massage it in before she gets up to walk!) Make sure to rub not just the bottom of the feet, but in between the toes, the back of the foot, and the ankles also.

Now that we've explored some of the ways to indulge in sensual pleasures, it's time to move. . . .

Deeper into the Realm of the Senses

When the girl begins to show her love by outward signs and motions, the lover should try to gain her over entirely by various ways and means.

—*Kama Sutra*

At its best, sex is like sitting in a jet waiting for it to take off to an eagerly anticipated location. Of course, you will have a better, more relaxing trip if you organize yourself beforehand so that you don't have to rush, don't have to second-guess yourself about whether you forgot something important on the mantelpiece at home. In the same way, once you lay a foundation for great sex through proper hygiene and proper grooming, you can concentrate on the ride, and anticipate the joys of arriving at the destination. You are not worried about odors, because the odors coming from you are the natural aromas of being heated up for sex, which act as aphrodisiacs. You are not worried about stale breath or about scraping your partner with an untrimmed nail from your big toe. You can concentrate on receiving pleasure and on giving pleasure. You can relax as you float into the transporting sensual pleasures.

> **It is said by some that there is no fixed time or order between the embrace, the kiss, and the pressing or scratching with the nails or fingers, but that all these things should be done generally before sexual union takes place. However, anything may take place at anytime, for love does not care for time or order.**
>
> —Kama Sutra

Even in this deeper level there are fundamentals, as put forth by the *Kama Sutra*. But it is also a time for the imagination to take flight. Perhaps a vibrator might be a pleasant adjunct for a husband and wife's sex date. Perhaps an impromptu dance with an ostrich-feather boa, which might find other uses later in the evening. And, in the beginning, middle, and end, there is the word. Sweet nothings whispered hot into the ear, or cried aloud at a peak moment. The moment of truth is near. Here are further lessons from the *Kama Sutra*, a journey toward getting to know ourselves on the most human level.

Embraces

In the *Kama Sutra* there are four different kinds of embraces: touching, piercing, rubbing, pressing.

Touching: When a man under some pretext or other goes in front of or alongside a woman and touches her body with his own, it is called the "touching embrace."

Piercing: When a woman in a lonely place bends down, as if to pick up something, and pierces, as it were, a man sitting or standing, with her breasts, and the man in return takes hold of them, it is called the "piercing embrace."

Rubbing: When two lovers are walking slowly together, either in the dark or in a place of public resort, or in a lonely place, and rub their bodies against each other, it is called the "rubbing embrace."

Pressing: When on the above occasion one of them presses the other's body forcibly against a wall or pillar, it is called the "pressing embrace."

There are four other types of embraces. The first two are performed standing:

Twining of a Creeper: When a woman, clinging to a man as a creeper twines round a tree, bends his head down to hers with the desire of kissing him and

> Even those embraces that are not mentioned in the *Kama Shastra* [another Indian commentary on love and sex] should be practiced at the time of sexual enjoyment, if they are in any way conducive to the increase of love or passion. The rules of the *Shastra* apply as long as the passion of man is middling, but when the wheel of love is once set in motion, there is then no *Shastra* and no order.
>
> — Kama Sutra

Twining of a Creeper

Climbing a Tree

slightly makes the sound of *Sut, sut,* embraces, and looks lovingly toward him, it is called "twining of a creeper."

Climbing a Tree: When a woman, having placed one of her feet on the foot of her lover, and the other one on his thighs, passes one of her arms around his back, and the other on his shoulders, makes slightly the sounds of singing and cooing, and wishes, as it were, to climb up him in order to have a kiss, it is called "climbing a tree."

These embraces take place during copulation:

Sesame and Rice: When lovers lie on a bed, and embrace each other so closely that the arms and thighs of one are encircled by the arms and thighs of the other, and are, as it were, rubbing up against them, this is called an embrace like "the mixture of sesame seed and rice."

> **If he does not perceive the woman's emotional state and, when he is burning with desire, begins his effusions without worrying about the woman's reaction, a man will always meet with failure. Neither he nor the woman will experience true satisfaction.**
>
> —Kama Sutra

Milk and Water: When a man and a woman are very much in love with each other, and, not thinking of pain or hurt, embrace each other as if they are entering into each other's bodies either while the woman is sitting on the lap of the man or in front of him, or on a bed, then it is called an embrace like a "mixture of milk and water."

The torso is not the only part of the body embraced. As passion heightens, the *Kama Sutra* shows how the embrace becomes more focused and more intense.

Embracing single members of the body:

Sesame and Rice

Embrace of Thighs: When one of two lovers presses forcibly one or both of the thighs of the other between his or her own, it is called the "embrace of thighs."

Embrace of the *jaghana,* that is, the part of the body from the navel downward to the thighs: When the man presses the *jaghana* of the woman's body against his own, and mounts upon her to practice, either scratching with the nail or finger, or biting or striking or kissing, the hair of the woman being loose and flowing, it is called the "embrace of the *jaghana.*"

Embrace of the Breasts: When a man places his breast between the breasts of a woman and presses her with it, it is called "embrace of the breasts." *This embrace has also been described as the woman being seated or lying over a man and settling her breasts onto his thighs, and then pressing her breasts and his thighs together.*

Embrace of the Forehead: When either of the lovers touches the mouth, the eyes, and the forehead of the other with his or her own, it is called "embrace of the forehead."

Milk and Water

Favorite hugs

I like to touch my partner, either a light touch on the arm, leg, neck . . . or other body parts while sitting together, while in bed, or holding hands while walking.   Rodney, 23

First embraces after long absence. Bear hugs. Light brushing over the top of the breast with clothes on.   Jesse, 21

Placing your head in the crook of the arm between the chest and armpit, with both arms hugging tight.   Elise, 39

I love caressing my partner's penis when we are just sitting together. I also love embracing when we sleep. That is my favorite.   Rose, 38

I love when a guy grabs my butt when we are kissing. That move will get me in bed so fast.   Bella, 26

To embrace him right out of the shower, with a little bit of wetness on him.   Amelia, 25

When my husband and I are lying in bed and I curve my body around his while we sleep. Phenomenal feeling.   Dorothy, 29

Snuggling that doesn't lead to sex.   Lois, 44

Arms around their upper back or neck so that my breast and his chest are touching.   Alma, 42

☙☙☙

I like when a man caresses my back when he kisses me. I like a man who moves his hands up and down the full length of my body.   Michelle, 29

☙☙☙

Spooning.   Isaac, 44

☙☙☙

I happen to like big beautiful men. Hugging a man with my face on his abdomen really turns me on. Some form of touching my beloved, be it arm, leg, shoulder, or hand, when he is near. Standing or lying down and being held is best of all. Caressing his back and also his rear while kissing sends me, also.   Alicia, 25

☙☙☙

I like to lock legs with my partner. Just lying down relaxing with my part-ner. I would do the rear-end clutching while making love.   Carolyn, 36

☙☙☙

My favorite is a full, strong chest-to-breast embrace.   Richard, 30

☙☙☙

I like touching in any way, holding hands, hand on arm, and hugging. I enjoy standing and holding around the waist or shoulders.   Eliza-beth, 42

☙☙☙

Some of the most romantic embraces are probably the most platonic ones. At a movie, walking hand in hand, or even just holding one another. These embraces in their simplicity allow you to reflect to your partner how much you care through the simple power of touch. Arthur, 30

◎◎◎

Holding hands while walking down the street. Cuddling up close on a train.   Patty, 27

◎◎◎

I love any kind of touching and holding that isn't crushing or hurtful. I really like to snuggle a woman in my arms, or hold her hips.   Harry, 38

◎◎◎

Yes, I am a butt woman. I like to caress my partner's rear.   Louise, 48

◎◎◎

I think I like a light brushing like when you are in the kitchen or in the bathroom and you just kind of brush up against the person from behind. I also like the tight embrace that you experience when you are kissing someone passionately. I just really like touching.   Sara, 30

◎◎◎

I like the hands on the face while sharing a passionate kiss. Another favorite is caressing the back of his head and neck while kissing. Paula, 48

◎◎◎

I wrap my arms around her waist, and subtly massage the small of her back.   Hiram, 27

◎◎◎

I create a tension between myself and mate, getting very close and nuzzling into the person. I hold him very close and stroke him lovingly. I place my legs so the other person's pelvis is very close to mine. I nuzzle slowly and gently and I very subtly undulate while holding him close. That's the passionate/sexy embrace. The warmth, intensity, and passion I exude turns the person on. I'm very sensitive to what people want and feel.   Justine, 47

My favorite embrace is when a big man approaches me from behind and gives me a hug . . . and pulls me to his chest. It is the most intimate hug in the world. I feel safe, secure, and loved.   Jacki, 37

Kissing

Kissing is one of the most potent forms of communication there is. Books have been written solely on that topic, and they all agree on one thing: A kiss is *never* just a kiss. It can be a Band-Aid. ("Does that make the boo-boo feel better?") It can be a warning ("You're gonna die. Soon!"), if we are to believe the Godfather films. Depending on who does it and why, it can be a platonic and informal greeting, like "Whazzz up, girl!" or it can be a platonic and formal hello. It can be a friendly and not so platonic "I'm glad to see you again." (Twinkle in the eyes!) It can be an emphatic "I wanna git with you. Now!" There are kisses that mean, "I'm sorry."

As opposed to some other preambles to lovemaking—massaging feet, for instance—a couple can kiss anywhere. Cars, alcoves during a sudden rain shower, a back room at a party. Parisians are well known for kissing on the street. There are kisses that are named for different nationalities: the Eskimo kiss, where the parties rub their noses against one another's; the gypsy kiss, where one partner gently breathes cigarette smoke into the other person's mouth. (A health-minded variant would be simply to breathe into the other person's open mouth.) There is the Trobriand kiss (the Trobriand Islands are located 1500 miles north of Sydney, Australia), which consists of sucking the lower lip, and, according to the early-twentieth-century anthropologist Bronislaw Malinowski, biting the partner's eyelashes, as passions rise. And of course there is the French kiss (also called "deep kiss" or "soul kiss"), in which tongues touch. It is probably the best-known kiss to most black Americans. With an excursion into this section of the *Kama Sutra*, we will learn a few more.

> **There are no special moments in which kissing, scratching, and biting should be employed, since they are constantly used in amorous relations and preliminaries.**
>
> —Kama Sutra

According to the *Kama Sutra* the prime places to plant a kiss are the forehead, the eyes, the cheeks, the throat, the bosom, the breasts, the lips, the interior of the mouth, the joints of the thighs, the arms, and the navel, the brow, the hair, the chest, the lower lips, the tongue, the thighs, the armpits, and the sex.

This is the first set of kisses described by the *Kama Sutra*:

1. The *Normal Kiss*: when a girl touches only the mouth of her lover with her own, but does not let herself do anything.

2. The *Throbbing Kiss*: when a girl, setting aside her bashfulness a little, wishes to touch the lip that is pressed into her mouth, and with that object moves her lower lip, but not the upper one.

3. The *Touching Kiss*: when a girl touches her lover's lip with her tongue and, having shut her eyes, places her hands on those of her lover.

The second set is comprised of the following kisses:

1. The *Straight Kiss*: when the lips of two lovers are brought into direct contact with each other.

2. The *Bent Kiss*: when the heads of two lovers are bent toward each other, and so bent kissing takes place.

3. The *Turned Kiss*: when one of them turns up the face of the other by holding the head and chin, and then kissing.

4. The *Pressed Kiss*: when the lower lip is pressed with much force.

The third set of kisses described in the *Kama Sutra* are:

> Whatever things may be done by one of the lovers to the other, the same should be returned by the other: that is, if the woman kisses him he should kiss her in return.
>
> —Kama Sutra

1. The *Gently Pressed Kiss*: effected by taking hold of the lower lip between two fingers and then, after touching it with the tongue, pressing it with great force with the lip.

2. The *Kiss of the Upper Lip*: when a man kisses the upper lip of a woman, while she in return kisses his lower lip.

3. *The Clasping Kiss*: when one of the lovers takes both lips of the other between his or her own. On the occasion of the kiss, if one of them touches the teeth, the tongue, and the palate of the other with his or her tongue, it is called "fighting of the tongue." In the same way, the pressing of the teeth of the one against the mouth of the other is to be practiced.

The fourth section of the *Kama Sutra* is comprised of the following:

Kissing is of four kinds: moderate, contacted, pressed, and soft, according to the different parts of the body that are kissed, or different kinds of kisses are appropriate for different parts of the body.

When a woman looks at the face of her lover while he is asleep, and kisses it to show her intention or desire, it is called a "Kiss That Kindles Love."

When a woman kisses her lover while she is engaged in business, or while he is quarreling with her, or while he is looking at something else, so that his mind may be turned away, it is called a "Kiss That Turns Away."

When a lover coming home late at night kisses his beloved who is asleep on her bed, in order to show her his desire, it is called a "Kiss That Awakens." On such an occasion the woman may pretend to be asleep at the time of her lover's arrival, so that she may know his intention and obtain respect from him.

When a person kisses the reflection of the person he loves in a mirror, in water, or on a wall, it is called a "Kiss Showing the Intention."

When a person kisses a child sitting on his lap, or a picture or an image or a figure, in the presence of the person beloved by him, it is called a "Transferred Kiss."

When at night at a theater . . . a man coming up to a woman kisses a finger of her hand if she is standing, or a toe of her foot if she be sitting, or when a woman in shampooing her lover's body places her face in his thighs (as if she were sleepy) so as to inflame his passion, and kisses his thigh or great toe, it is called a "Demonstrative Kiss."

The Kissing Game: A wager may be laid as to which will get hold of the lips of the first. If the woman loses, she should pretend to cry, should keep her lover off by shaking her hands, and turn away from him and dispute with him saying, "Let another wager be laid." If she loses this a second time, she should appear doubly distressed, and when her lover is off his guard or asleep, she should get hold of his lower lip, and hold it in her teeth, so that it should not slip away; and then she should laugh, make a loud noise, deride him, dance about, and say whatever she likes in a joking way, moving her eyebrows, and rolling her eyes.

—Kama Sutra

Amid the talk of all of the varieties of kissing and embracing and oral sex and sexual positions, there remains one supreme question: Does your partner like what you are doing to him or her during your most intimate moments? Do you like what your partner is doing to you during those moments? If not, how do you get in synch with one another's sexual needs and desires? The simplest answer is communication. But as with all things in sex, timing is everything.

> However expert a man may be in arts and science, however famous and important, if he is scorned by women in the art of love, he is a dead man.
>
> —Kama Sutra

"When I was in college, I was making out with a woman and I blew into her ear," said Matt, 46, a real estate broker in Savannah, Georgia. "Apparently she either didn't like it or didn't like the way I was doing it. Anyway, she suddenly pulled back and said sharply, 'Stop it!' I was shocked, not sure exactly what, if anything, I did wrong. The mood for love had certainly passed, and the evening ended with an argument and me angrily leaving the room over— I think it was over what kind of food we should have delivered."

How might the situation have been handled?

"Well, as it turned out, a couple of months later I was with another woman and tried blowing in her ear also," Matt continued. "She didn't like the way I was doing it either, but rather than scolding me, she gently pulled back and muttered softly, 'uh-uh,' meaning no." Later that evening she told me that she did like a zephyr around her ear lobes, but said I was doing it 'a bit too hard.' She drew close and demonstrated my technique on me. It sounded like a hurricane! Having had it demonstrated on me, I marveled that I hadn't blown out someone's eardrum over the years. Then she showed me how she liked it: mouth shut, breath lightly coming through the nose in little pants, and never directly into the ear canal.

"I didn't necessarily need a demonstration of how what I did felt," Matt added. "But she was gentle in telling me that what I was doing was wrong for her and gentle in telling me what she liked and how she liked it."

Notice also how she provided her bit of instruction outside the context of their intimacy. She was respectful of his feelings and also got what she wanted.

Sandee, a 32-year-old bank clerk from Chattanooga, Tennessee, said one evening her boyfriend had lubricated his finger and was playing with the entrance to her anus.

"It was at the end of a long evening of making love, and he was just rubbing his lubricated finger there. We had discussed it before in a general sort of way, and so when he started doing it I wasn't surprised. In fact, I welcomed it. But when I tried to do it to him, he pulled away gently. He then told me that in principle he had nothing against me probing him there—he wasn't the kind of straight man who felt that if he enjoyed anal play from a woman it meant that he was a latent homosexual. But he said that as a matter of personal comfort, he would prefer that we do it during or after a shower. He said at such times he would feel cleaner, and therefore freer and less self-conscious. If we were in the full heat of fucking the way we had been about an hour beforehand, just pulling away would have been sufficient. But we were just mellowing out, and so the explanation of *why* he pulled away was not intrusive."

The one thing that everyone says about expressing your desires is to be gentle. Don't rebuke. Don't berate. Don't be cruel. If you pull your partner's hand to initiate a certain motion you like, don't yank his or her hand to the spot. Guide it toward you or evade it or push it away tenderly. And there are creative ways to let your desires be known.

"I had one girlfriend who started touching her own clitoris or breasts," said Oliver, 28, an advertising accounts executive from Boston. "After doing that awhile, she'd pull my hand, meaning that I should imitate her. It was a real turn-on watching her masturbate and then taking over. I was secure in knowing that she liked what I was doing, because she was guiding it. She wasn't expecting me to be a mind reader. It really added to our erotic life."

Sex manuals such as *SoulMates*, or books of erotic fiction, certain kinds of pornography—even writing or e-mailing one another—can be useful ways to communicate sexual desires discreetly but plainly, and to prod sexual boundaries. But here's a reminder: Not every fantasy *must* be acted out in reality. Just because your girlfriend said she wants a threesome with you and another woman, doesn't mean that you have to plan one. In sober moments, make sure that it is something you really want to do. Often a fantasy in and of itself can add fuel to your sex life.

Finally, remember to laugh. Remember that as transporting as sex can be, and as pleasurable, it can also be ridiculous. So be sure to laugh. Not *at* one another, but *with* one another. It is sure to bring you closer.

"My husband and I were fucking all over our loft one time," said Eve, 30, a hospital administrator in Saratoga Springs, New York. "We started off in the bedroom, moved to the living room, made love in the shower, then moved to the kitchen. He lifted me onto a long wood food preparation table we had. When we started fucking on it, somehow air got caught in my back, creating a vacuum so that every time I arched toward him, parting my back from the wood made a farting sound. We tried to ignore it at first, but the sound happened too frequently and it was too funny! We laughed. Yes, it broke the mood, but we somehow felt psychically closer. And then we moved to the dining area and picked up where we left off."

Favorite kisses

What made him so good is that he could match my kissing ability. . . . I am a passionate kisser. I kiss the lips, the tongue, suck on the tongue and lips.   Kendra, 19

☙☙☙

A full-lipped kiss, with the right amount of saliva. Not too much, not too dry. It was long and passionate.   Maria, 39

☙☙☙

The best kisser I've ever been with used to rub my face when we kissed. He also liked kissing when we had sex. . . . I try to follow my partner's lead in terms of what he likes. If he is using his tongue, then I use tongue. If he touches and caresses, I do the same.   Angela, 38

☙☙☙

I love a little nibble on the bottom lip. Not too wet, not too dry. Guy, 36

☙☙☙

The best kisser I know is slow and gentle, but hungry at the same time. And will leave no mess.   Lorna, 25

☙☙☙

Lips that seem to match, tongue kissing that's smooth and sensual. Nice soft, smooth lips.   Enid, 42

☙☙☙

The best kisser I had was very erotic. Meaning sucking my bottom lip, sucking my tongue, taking his time kissing you erotically and passionately.   Pauline, 29

☙☙☙

A man whispered sweet nothings in my ear, nibbled my ear, kissed my entire face except my lips. The anticipation was mind boggling. Then he gently, slowly sucked my lips. French-kissed, then pulled my bottom lip. I almost fainted. The gentleness, yet passionate way in which he kissed, also having me wait, and yearn for him to French-kiss (pull and suck on my tongue) heightened the pleasure.   Claudia, 33

ⓖⓖⓖ

The person that taught me to kiss would swallow before kissing, which caused his mouth not to be full of saliva. He would kiss me all over my face and make a smacking sound.   Emily, 24

ⓖⓖⓖ

The best kisser I ever had was my ex-girlfriend. Her kisses were not only powerful, but deliberate. She knew when to be soft, hard, compliant, masterful.   Clarence, 30

ⓖⓖⓖ

He started out with full-lipped kisses that were deep and slow. Slowly penetrated my mouth with his tongue. Wasn't too wet and drippy or noisy.   Toni, 27

ⓖⓖⓖ

I've discovered that chewing gum really makes it for me. Spit out the gum first, but the sweetness, the freshness of the taste, is a real turn-on while kissing!   Jason, 38

ⓖⓖⓖ

Ex-boyfriend—when he wanted to be intimate, his kisses were so tender. He kissed full, but very lightly to the point that we were only touching tongues . . . that set me on fire.   Imani, 26

ⓖⓖⓖ

A man once took the time to kiss every inch of my lips and my face without sticking his tongue down my throat. It was a total, total perfect moment . . . so when the tongue came, it was a glorious experience. Very sweet. Not too sloppy. Not too wet. Just very sensual and nice.   Erin, 37

The *Kama Sutra* on Pressing or Marking or Scratching with the Nails

When love becomes intense, pressing with the nails or scratching the body with them is practiced. . . . But pressing with the nails is not a usual thing except with those who are intensely passionate. The places that are to be pressed with the nails are: the armpit, the throat, the breasts, the lips, the *jaghana*, and the thighs.

1. *Sounding:* when a person presses the chin, the breasts, the lower lip, or the *jaghana* of another so softly that no scratch or mark is left, but only the hair on the body becomes erect from the touch of the nails, and the nails themselves make a sound.

2. *Half-moon*: The curved mark with the nails, which is impressed on the neck and the breasts, is called the "half-moon."

3. *A Circle*: When the half-moons are impressed opposite each other, it is called a "circle." This mark with the nails is generally made on the navel, the small cavities about the buttocks, and on the joints of the thigh.

4. *A Line*: a mark in the form of a small line, which can be made on any part of the body.

5. *A Tiger's Nail or Claw:* This same line, when it is curved, and made on the breast, is called a "tiger's nail."

6. *A Peacock's Foot:* When a curved mark is made on the breast by means of the five nails, it is called a "peacock's foot." This mark is made with the object of being praised, for it requires a great deal of skill to make it properly.

7. *The Jump of a Hare:* When five marks with the nails are made close to one another near the nipple of the breast, it is called "the jump of a hare."

8. *The Leaf of a Blue Lotus:* A mark made on the breast or on the hips in the form of a leaf of the blue lotus is called the "leaf of the blue lotus."

The *Kama Sutra* on Biting

All the places that can be kissed are also the places that can be bitten, except the upper lip, the interior of the mouth, and the eyes.

The Hidden Bite: the biting which is shown only by the excessive redness of the skin that is bitten.

The Swollen Bite: when the skin is pressed down on both sides.

The Point: when a small portion of the skin is bitten with two teeth only.

The Line of Points: when such small portions of the skin are bitten with all the teeth.

The Coral and the Jewel: The biting that is done by bringing together the teeth and the lips is called the "coral and the jewel." The lips are the coral, and the teeth are the jewel.

The Line of Jewels: when biting is done with all the teeth.

The Broken Cloud: The biting that consists of many broad rows of marks near to one another, and with red intervals, is call the "biting of a boar." This is impressed on the breasts and the shoulders; and these two last modes of biting are peculiar to persons of intense passion.

Love at first bite?

Yes, I bite and like to be bitten . . . gently . . . nibbled. It is a regular part of my sexual encounter.   LaDel, 19

ᠪᠪᠪ

I like biting nipples, that's about it. It is not done enough for me to say it is part of my sexual repertoire.   Helen, 38

ᠪᠪᠪ

Being bitten is good if it's sensual, if it causes no pain, but is done in a teasing way. I am not into pain in sex.   Monica, 44

ᠪᠪᠪ

Light nibbling is okay, but not a regular part of my sex play.   Cheyenne, 42

ᠪᠪᠪ

Yes, I like when a man nibbles on my ear.   Teresa, 29

ᠪᠪᠪ

I like to gently bite and be gently bitten. It has occasionally been part of my sex play. Sometimes it flows that way. I would advise to make sure the moans are from pleasure.   Richelle, 25

ᠪᠪᠪ

I don't like pain in any form.   Jon, 44

ᠪᠪᠪ

I don't like bites. I bruise very easily and think it looks hideous. Roberta, 36

ᠪᠪᠪ

I don't like to be bitten. There are too many diseases out there to be opening wounds on people.   Brad, 36

Biting is fine if it is done at low intensity. Don't break the skin. Don't leave teeth marks.   Joe, 23

❧❧❧

I nibble occasionally. I would say be very careful and don't do it on the really sensitive parts.   Lewis, 27

❧❧❧

I would have to say no. I don't bite or scratch and I don't want it to be done to me. I think it could lead to more aggressive sex, and that isn't what I want.   Frances, 30

❧❧❧

I do, but the key to nibbling is the pressure used. I like eating jelly beans or Mike and Ikes. You don't want to clamp down on the gummy candy because it gets all caught in your teeth, and you miss out on the flavor because it's such a lightly flavored candy. The same is applicable for nipples or flesh. I delicately bite, then use my strong tongue to lick and massage the bitten place.   Lester, 39

❧❧❧

I don't want to be bitten or scratched, unless it is lightly along the back. Noel, 33

❧❧❧

What needs to be remembered is that you are not eating ribs. Bites should be a small amount of skin in your lover's most sensitive zones, nipping a little.   Rhona, 46

Striking and Aural Sex

The *Kama Sutra* has an understated S & M aspect, where instead of being laid over your lover's lap and swatted across the buttocks with either an open hand or a paddle, there are blows to the shoulders, the space between the breasts, the sides, and the back, delivered with the back of the hand (the fingers a little contracted), the fist, and the open palm of the hand. Each of these blows has a special mouth sound associated with it that the woman emits—the thundering sound, the cooing sound, the weeping sound, and the sounds *Hin, Phut, Phat* (an imitation of the sound of bamboo being split), *Sut,* and *Plat* (like the sound of something falling into water). The *Kama Sutra* says, for instance, that "while the woman is engaged in congress the space between the breasts should be struck with the back of the hand, slowly at first, and then proportionately to the increasing excitement until the end. . . . At this time the sounds *Hin* and others may be made. . . ."

It continues: "During the excitement, when the woman is not accustomed to striking, she continually utters words expressive of prohibition, sufficiency, or desire of liberation, as well as the words *father, mother,* intermingled with the sighing, weeping, and thundering sound. Toward the conclusion of the congress the breasts, the *jaghana,* and the sides of the woman should be pressed with the open palms of the hand, with some force, until the end of it, and then sounds like those of the quail or the goose should be made."

And so said the *Kama Sutra.* And so says contemporary America.

Before we get into how edgy sexual practices have leached into the modern mainstream American scene, we should define our terms. The edgy folks whose sensibilities have made their way to the center of America's consciousness are members of what is commonly called the BDSM community. The letters stand for Bondage and Dominance (sometimes Discipline) and Sadism and Masochism. Another common and more general term used to describe the community is Dominance and Submission.

As multifarious as the terms might be, the activities of the people who fall under the category are even more so. The most basic component, however, is that one person places him- or herself under the power of another in an erotic, if not out and out sexual, context. One person is controlled, the other controls. This dynamic may manifest itself in role-play as teacher/student, slave/master, king/concubine, or any number of other scenarios. The dynamic might also be exhibited in one partner restricting the movements of another with rope, handcuffs, scarves, or other materials. Frequently, but not always, the person who is bound is teased or stimulated with feathers, furs, or simply the right touch of the hand.

Another way of displaying dominance is by administering pain. The dominant, the sadist, might inflict pain—or a sensation in that gray area between pain and pleasure—in any number of ways. He or she might do something as mild as tickle the partner, or ratchet up the erotic sensation by placing clothespins on the partner's nipples or foreskin. Swatting with a paddle or using whips or riding crops are also common options. Sometimes the sadist doesn't touch his or her partner. Instead, the pain is inflicted through verbal humiliation or haranguing.

It is beyond the purview of this book to discuss the pros and cons of such behavior, or for that matter to pass judgment on it. Let us say for now that what might be considered normal human sexual behavior has a broad range. But in stretching the boundaries of any activity, common sense should be the order of the day.

Don't indulge in this kind of play unless you know the person. It is not the stuff of casual acquaintanceships and one-night stands. The more extreme the play, the better you should know your partner. Also, always have a "safe word," that is, a verbal signal that indicates things have gone uncomfortably far and you want the game to *stop*. Be sure to make the word something other than the word "stop." Perhaps a color. One person I knew used a catlike hissing sound to mean, "Stop! I am no longer into this!"

In terms of tying up your partner, be careful not to cut off circulation by tying too tightly or at crucial circulation points in the body. Finally, be very careful with having any bodily fluids coming into direct contact with mucus membranes. Such contact can lead to any number of diseases, including AIDS. Better yet, before embarking on any heavy BDSM activities, read some of the numerous books that specialize in those practices.

Mild versions of S&M have been virtually mainstreamed, some have literally gone prime time. Look at black leather pants and some jewelry that you can find on the arms of the straightest mothers of Jack and Jill. Flashes of S&M, B&D, can be seen in news shows and jokes on family-hour television shows. But given the black historical connotation of sex, bondage, and violence—not to mention the nation's concern with domestic violence—how comfortable are African Americans with S&M elements in their role playing? Is it a regular part of our sexual repertoire, and if so, did we have initial problems playing those games, given our historical context?

How do blacks relate to black-and-blue?

Not a regular part of my sex life. When so, my hands were loosely bound with a scarf and I could easily get out of it.   Tamika, 24

I like the spankings that are a regular part of our sexual repertoire. We tried S&M/B&D once or twice, but we both had a problem going real deep with the bondage. We are both very African centered and after talking about it we came to the conclusion our knowledge of the slave experience played a major role in our feelings.   Valerie, 38

I have not tried S&M or B&D. Maybe I'm wrong for thinking this, but I don't think too much about slavery or any other political/social issues while engaging in sexual matters.   Wanda, 26

No, but might try it.   Lois, 44

Never engaged in S&M sex. Mild forms of domination/submission. Infrequent occasions of bondage . . . mental adjustments had to be made, but this has less to do with history and politics and more to do with simply trusting someone not to harm you or go too far while you are tied down. I like tying down a man using imaginary ties—that is, you tell him he's loosely tied with imaginary ropes, he can look, but not touch, no matter what is being done to him. This is sexier in my opinion.   Alma, 38

⬡⬡⬡

I have on occasion blindfolded him and tied him to the bed. Never really thought about history of slavery and so forth while doing it.   Nia, 26

⬡⬡⬡

Used handcuffs a few times, in a playful manner.   Malcolm, 38

⬡⬡⬡

I find bondage and beatings a bad flash from the past.   Maya, 46

⬡⬡⬡

Every now and then we do the tying up and blindfolding, but that might be about as far as we take it. No pain! You only do things like that with someone you totally trust.   Yvette, 26

Oral Sex

Jokes about blacks and oral sex, or perhaps more accurately, blacks and their lack of appetite for oral sex, are legion. There is some rumbling about black women not performing fellatio. But the biggest ruckus comes from black men saying that they haven't, don't, and won't perform cunnilingus on a woman. At least that was what they said in public. Is it still true? Was it ever true? And if it is true, do we perform it well and with enthusiasm? Or are we reluctant lovers in that regard because of some cultural prohibition? Our respondents weigh in on the subject, after words from the *Kama Sutra* on oral sex. Alas, only tech-

103

niques for fellatio are given. Sorry, ladies. Remember that India was a patriarchal society around the time of Christ, when they think the *Kama Sutra* was written. The only guidance the manual gives to men wanting to perform cunnilingus is this: "The way of kissing the yoni [vagina] should be known from kissing the mouth." That is all. But, perhaps if perfectly executed, it is enough.

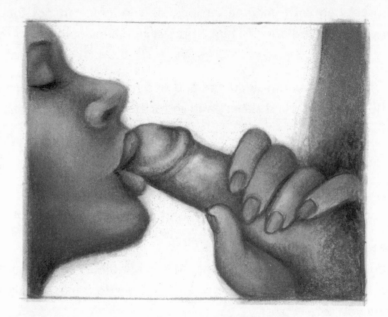

The *Kama Sutra* on Oral Congress

1. The nominal congress: holding the man's lingam with hand and placing it between lips, moving the mouth about.

2. Biting the sides: covering the end of the lingam with fingers collected together like the bud of a plant or flower, pressing the sides of it with lips, using teeth.

3. Pressing outside: pressing the end of the lingam with lips closed together, kissing it as if trying to draw it out.

4. Pressing inside: putting the lingam farther into the mouth, pressing it with the lips, and then taking it out.

5. Kissing: holding the lingam in the hand, kissing it as if kissing the lower lip.

6. Rubbing: touching the tongue to every part of the lingam, and passing the tongue over the end of it.

7. Sucking a mango fruit: putting half of the lingam into the mouth, forcibly kissing and sucking it.

8. Swallowing up: putting the whole lingam into the mouth, pressing it to the very end, as if going to swallow the tip.

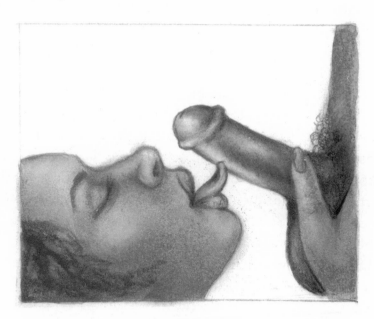

The stereotype is that black people don't engage in oral sex. Is this true . . . ?

I have only had one partner in my sexual experience who would not perform oral sex on me, but wanted it performed on him. I enjoy performing it. It would hurt the relationship if they wanted me to perform oral sex on them, but not vice versa.   Nessa, 28

ꂦꂦꂦ

My husband says that all black men do it, but lie about it. In my limited experience I would say this is true.   Nicole, 39

ꂦꂦꂦ

I have a male friend who says he'd rather perform oral sex than have "regular intercourse." He says it is just as satisfying. I love pleasing my partner in this manner. It is a different type of sensation. and I love having my partner lick and suck on my pussy—that is, if they know what they are doing. I have, however, been with guys who said they did not do it or like having it done to them. The worst oral sex session I had was when someone acted as if they were afraid to really lick and taste me. He seemed to touch it slightly and almost jump back from me as if he might be bitten. The best I've ever had was someone who seemed to put his heart and soul into the whole thing. He opened me up and licked long and slow. He also nibbled my clit and then buried his face in my pussy. He fingered me while he was doing all this. It was great. Most men think a woman wants them to go on and on. *Wrong!!* They need to hit it right for a while, then let it go.   Helen, 38

ꂦꂦꂦ

It seems to me that every black person does it. I do it and love it because I like to see my boyfriend happy. I don't mind receiving it, but I prefer penetration.   Mattie, 26

I have performed it, but I really don't enjoy it. It is for the other person's pleasure, when I do it. I have to admit, however, that I like it being performed on me. But if someone didn't want to perform it on me, it really wouldn't affect our relationship. I simply would not perform oral on him. In terms of best and worst, the worst was a guy who just slobbered all over it. The best was a guy who took his time and really felt like he was enjoying it as much as I was.   Georgia, 25

⬥⬥⬥

A few years ago my black friends would not admit that they participated in oral sex. Now they will admit it quietly, and play it down. I enjoy doing it with my husband, and I love when he does it to me. Not getting oral would hurt my relationship with the guy. Most men who won't still expect the woman to perform oral sex. I cannot be with such a man. The best oral sex was with a guy who knew how to treat my clitoris. Biting the clitoris is a no-no. Lick it, gently suck on it, but do not chew it like gum.   Ruby, 29

⬥⬥⬥

I think that most black people like oral sex. But my husband doesn't. How sad. I try performing it on my husband, but he just isn't into it. I absolutely love it being performed on me, but when he has tried to perform it on me, I make him stop. I don't think he is really enjoying himself. You have to like it to be good at it. It has to be part of who you are. Luckily our sex life is strong without it. In the past I've had men bite, blow, or pull down there. Just thinking about it is painful. The best was so good because he performed like there was nothing better in the world. He told me how good I tasted, how good I smelled.   Kendra, 44

⬥⬥⬥

Black folks do it and do it well. I've never had anyone say no to performing it on me. And I enjoy performing it. I like it being performed on me.

To the extent there has been any reluctance, it usually has to do with hygiene, which is easy to take care of. Men who aren't adept at it are still pretty good at taking instruction—learning to kiss the outside, how to lick, how to suck. But there was this brother who needed no instruction. Not only did he know how to kiss, lick, suck, on my vagina and clit, but also my butt. Whew. Blew my mind.   Susan, 42

ⓒⓒⓒ

None of the black men I have been with have inhibitions about oral sex. I enjoy doing it because it pleases my partner, and I enjoy it being done to me, but only if they have technique. They have to know how to suck my clitoris. Another thing most men do not do is take their time to really please you.   Malikah, 29

ⓒⓒⓒ

I think it depends on the generation. My generation and under, it is common practice. I believe the fifty and older probably do it, but just won't admit it. I do perform oral sex and I do enjoy it. The pleasure the man gets heightens my own. Since I did not always like doing it, it gives me satisfaction knowing I learned certain techniques and apparently learned them well. I love oral sex being performed on me and would not get involved with someone who does not like performing oral sex. Men should understand that when it is performed for extensive lengths of time, it can lead to soreness. It's best when the entire body is kissed first, a tease, but never kissing the clitoris. Then going for the gusto and kissing of the inner thighs can drive a woman crazy.   Gwen, 28

ⓒⓒⓒ

I find that back in the 1970s and through the early 1980s men would not admit doing it, although they were privately doing it. Now it is no longer a hidden intimacy. Personally, I do not enjoy performing oral sex. But I can't lie, I love it when it is done on me. That said, it wouldn't hurt

the relationship if they didn't do it. I don't expect anyone to do something to me that I would not want to do to them. The best oral sex is the
unexpected kind, when you thought he was going to do something else,
and then feel this unexpected surge.   Sherry, 36

666

I have and do perform oral sex, but only on special people. Whether I
like it performed on me depends on the quality of the oral sex being
performed. If a woman doesn't know what she is doing, then I'll just tell
her to stop. Usually when someone is not very good, it just means that
they don't like doing it.   Philip, 30

666

When I was married we did it. Giving and receiving was enjoyable. The
worst times are when a man is too rough, or has scratchy whiskers, or is
biting too hard. The best is light touching.   Irma, 42

666

Many of my friends engage in oral sex. I enjoy giving it tremendously,
and of course, like any man, enjoy receiving it. The best time was when
the woman had a tongue that seemed to be made of silk. It was as if she
knew the male penis like the back of her hand. The worst time was a
woman who used her teeth. Most people don't know how to perform
oral sex because they go at it from what they have heard or seen. It is an
art to be studied.   Travis, 30

666

I think a few years ago that was the case. Now it seems like it's more of
the norm. I perform oral sex, but the only reason I enjoy it is that I know
how much my boyfriend enjoys it. I enjoy it done on me only if it is done
correctly. It's not really a huge part of my sex life. In fact, it sometimes is
a turnoff for me.   Jill, 26

I've only been with my husband and I have to beg to get some.
Sharon, 43

※

Everyone I know does it—though I do know some women who only like receiving, but they still perform it. I enjoy performing it, and enjoy receiving it, when it is done correctly. Most people are not good at it because they are just licking and sucking without direction. They need to figure out what's down there and pay special attention to each part. The best for me was when this guy listened to my body's reactions and adjusted accordingly. He did not immediately stop and try to penetrate just because I had reached orgasm.   Ella, 27

※

I like performing it very, very much and enjoy receiving. I think women are too timid. They worry too much about how they're being judged. I appreciate it when a woman takes it and does what she wants to please herself. I like to watch her have fun. And I like the feel when they caress and take their time, not necessarily doing anything, but just playing around—stroking, sucking—whatever.   William, 38

※

My experience is that black people do engage in oral sex. Some don't like to admit it, but believe me they do. Although, I have a girlfriend that didn't like to give or receive and that became an obstacle in our relationship. But most women I know love it as well as men. I love performing oral sex. I like to see the satisfaction that my partner gets from receiving oral sex from me. One guy I was with just kind of used the tip of his tongue, licking here and there. I could barely feel a thing. It was not enjoyable. The best I've had didn't just use his tongue, he used his hands, body . . . everything. He touched, caressed, the whole nine. He didn't just concentrate on the clit. He was all over the place. It was wonderful.   Cindy, 30

Hittin' the Skins

It is only when she is certain that she is truly loved and that her lover is indeed devoted to her, and will not change his mind, that she should give herself up to him. —*Kama Sutra*

Some call sexual intercourse the pièce de résistance of what we have been discussing throughout this entire book. We've had the appetizers, now to the main course, they would say. For others, however, penetration is just another course in the banquet of a sensually fulfilling life. And for still others sexual intercourse, penetration, is only the beginning. . . .

The *Kama Sutra* on Positions for Sexual Intercourse

The *Kama Sutra* categorizes men and women into three groups, according to the size of their genitals. Men from smallest to largest are hare, bull, horse; women from smallest to largest are deer, mare, elephant. The best sexual unions, the *Kama Sutra* says, are the unions of like—hare and deer, bull and mare, horse and elephant. But there are ways of maximizing pleasure, the *Kama Sutra* says, by wisely employing the various positions. For instance, when a man is bigger than the woman, the *Kama Sutra* recommends the woman "lie down in such a way as to widen her yoni," or vagina. If a woman with a large vagina is trying to accommodate a smaller man, the *Kama Sutra* suggests the woman choose a position in which she can "lie down so as to contract her yoni." It recommends these positions for a woman who is larger than the ideal size for her partner. But experiment to see how strict you need to be in your life.

> At last, when he knows the state of her feeling by her outward manner and conduct toward him ... he should begin to enjoy her when she is alone, for Vatsayayana lays it down that women, when resorted to at proper times and in proper places, do not turn away from their lovers.
>
> —Kama Sutra

The *Kama Sutra* is legendary for its multitude of sexual positions, but one has to remember that often the difference in position is merely raising a leg from the bed into the air. The *Kama Sutra* was not PC or liberated by our twenty-first-century American standards. In lying-down positions it is assumed the man is on top. In keeping with the artistic cast prominent in the *Kama Sutra*, the postures can be seen as part of a dance, moving from one position, crossing the legs, uncrossing them, then curling a leg to create yet another position. The result is not only outwardly balletic, but creates subtle changes of physical sensations and psychological states, resulting in a psychic dance of pleasure. Here are some of the basic lying and sitting postures described in the *Kama Sutra*:

The Position of Indrani

1. *The Widely Opened Position*: Essentially, this is the missionary position. The *Kama Sutra* recommends that the woman raise her pelvis with a pillow underneath her buttocks, and perhaps use "an unguent" to make penetration easier.

2. *The Yawning Position*: Here the woman is on her back and raises her thighs and keeps them wide apart so that they resemble a V, while the man, kneeling, is inside her.

3. *The Position of Indrani*: In this posture the woman is on her back, with her thighs drawn up to her breasts. As the man kneels to enter her, the soles of her feet are pressed to his belly. The *Kama Sutra* cautions that this position "is learned only by practice." Indrani was the wife of the Hindu god Indira. He was the ruler of the gods in early Vedic writings, similar to Zeus of the Greeks. Like Zeus, and Shango, a deity of the Yoruba peoples of West Africa, Indira was in charge of rain, lightning, and thunder.

The following positions should flow like a dance, as the couple press their bodies together with greater and greater ardor:

1. *The Clasping Position*, which is also called the Box position, is when the legs of both the male and the female are stretched straight out over each other. It is of two kinds: with the couples on their sides, or with the woman lying on her back. When the man is on top of the woman, his legs should be on the inside of her thighs. Some commentaries advise the woman to open and close her legs while the man is inside her, thereby causing ecstatic changes in her grip on the penis. This position is sometimes recommended when the man's penis is not large enough to accommodate the woman, but I'm sure any persons would find this posture enjoyable for the

The *Kama Sutra* on using the penis during intercourse

1. When the organs are brought together properly and directly, it is called "moving the organ forward."

2. When the lingam is held with the hand, and turned all round in the yoni, it is called a "churning."

3. When the yoni is lowered, and the upper part of it is struck with the lingam, it is called "piercing."

4. When the same thing is done on the lower part of the yoni, it is called "rubbing."

5. When the yoni is pressed by the lingam for a long time, it is called "pressing."

6. When the lingam is removed to some distance from the yoni, and then forcibly strikes it, it is called "giving a blow."

7. When only one part of the yoni is rubbed with the lingam, it is called the "blow of a boar."

8. When both sides of the yoni are rubbed in this way, it is called the "blow of a bull."

9. When the lingam is in the yoni, and is moved up and down frequently, and without being taken out, it is called "sporting of a sparrow." This takes place at the end of congress.

The Half-Pressed Position

The Crab

psychological intimacy it engenders. Employed on its side, this position makes for rather shallow penetration, but the intertwining of limbs makes for exquisite intimacy.

2. *The Pressing Position,* in which the "the woman presses her lover with her thighs." As she does this, she will bring her lover deeper into her body/piditaka.

3. *The Twining Position (envelopment):* is when the woman places one of her thighs across the thighs of her lover and presses, making for still greater penetration.

The following should flow together, dancelike. The repetition of the name "Yawning Position" is because this part of the *Kama Sutra* was inserted by a commentator:

1. *The Rising Position* is when the female raises both of her thighs straight up.

2. *The Yawning Position:* This position follows logically from the last, in that when the woman raises her legs, she will ultimately want to rest the backs of her ankles on the man's shoulders. This transforms the Rising Position into the Yawning Position. The man will probably want to hold her shins to keep her legs in place, as he kneels behind her. This position produces lots of friction between the penis and vagina when the woman's thighs are squeezed together.

3. *The Pressed Position:* Is similar to the Indrani Position, except that the soles of the woman's feet are more on the man's chest than his belly, and her thighs are not as compacted to her breast.

4. *The Half-Pressed Position:* As one might expect with this name, this position flows from—or into—the pressed po-

sition. In the Half-Pressed only one of her legs is pressed to the man's chest, while the other is stretched out. Some commentaries recommend alternating the legs at regular intervals, so that the end result resembles riding a bicycle.

5. *The Splitting of the Bamboo Position:* This posture is a continuance of the previous two. It occurs when the woman places one outstretched leg on her lover's shoulder. The *Kama Sutra* says to do this alternately, over and over. Again, the varying pressure caused by the raising and lowering of alternate legs produces a deep erotic sensation. This position might take some practice, too, along with a keen familiarity with one's cardiovascular fitness.

6. *The Fixing of a Nail Position:* This requires a bit of limberness on the woman's part. While on her back, she places one of her legs so that the heel touches her partner's forehead as he kneels and thrusts inside her.

7. *The Crab Position:* In this posture the man, kneeling, takes the woman as she is on her back, and she rests her feet on his hips and upper thighs.

8. *The Lotuslike Position:* In this one the woman is on her back with her legs folded, as if she were sitting cross-legged, and the man kneels and enters her exposed vagina. If the woman is flexible enough, she can probably try a full lotus position.

9. *The Turning Position:* This position is described by the *Kama Sutra* like this: "When a man, during congress, turns round, and enjoys the woman without leaving her, while she embraces him round the back all the time, it is called the 'turning position,' and is learned only by practice."

The Fixing of a Nail

Slip and Slide

K-Y jelly has given sexual lubricants a bad name. The gloppy, medicinal-smelling concoction that is most often associated with the gynecologist's examination room and shiny stainless steel instruments (which themselves look like something from the Spanish Inquisition) is one reason why many people hear the word "lubricant" and run for the hills.

Another reason lubricants have gotten a bad name is vanity. Men often feel that the use of a lube is a blow to their ego. After all, many men think, if you know the first thing about sex, then you ought to be able to make a woman flow like the Nile, right?

Women too may feel resorting to a lube is an admission of failure. If I am a real woman, she might think, shouldn't I be wet as the Florida Everglades after a few minutes of concerted clitoral massage? Isn't a lack of natural sexual lubricant a sign of some medical or maybe even emotional or psychological problem?

As a result of such thinking, most couples soldier on with their sex lives without lubes, complaining the next day, sometimes with mock delight, about how sore they are. No pain no gain, right?

Well, they needn't look at it that way. Feeling silky smooth and raring to go at it again the next day can be sexy, too. The use of a good lubricant might enhance their sex lives and bring more real joy than the bragging rights of the post-sex vaginal burn.

Let's start with a bit of myth-busting first: Lack of natural self-lubrication is not necessarily an indication of an inept lover or an undersexed woman. It is also not necessarily an indication of a physical or psychological problem. It's most often an inconvenience, one that many couples experience. It's also easily remedied.

Rest your minds about this one. The amount of natural lubrication created during sexual excitement is as variable as penis and clitoris size. Some women can be quite turned on and produce relatively little fluid; others, so much that they leave a wet spot the size of a manhole cover. It is a mistake to measure sexual excitement by how much lubricant a woman produces on her own. A woman's self-lubrication can vary depending on hormonal balances based on where she is in her menstrual cycle as well as other factors, emotional stress, her age, the use of prescription or illegal drugs, and so forth. Paradoxically, sustained foreplay or a long love-making session can also deplete a woman's natural lubrication.

As for the gloppy, foul-smelling problem, K-Y jelly has for some time been superseded by a number of other products that have the smooth feel of lotion and melt into the skin rather than leave a viscous residue. There are basically three kinds of lubes:

1. Petroleum-based lubes, such as petroleum jelly (Vaseline), baby oil, and mineral oil
2. Natural oil-based lubes, including items that you might more commonly find in your pantry—butter, Crisco, olive oil, peanut oil and the like

3. Water-based lubes: Probe, Astro-glide, Liquid Silk, and a number of other brands currently available on the market

Of the three kinds of lubricants, water-based lubes are by far the most popular and the most practical. Petroleum-based lubricants quickly (often in less than 60 seconds) make birth-control and prophylactic items, such as cervical caps and diaphragms, or condoms ineffective. Plus they can irritate the lining of the vagina and are difficult to wash off the body or bedclothes.

Water-based lubricants, on the other hand, do not affect birth-control and prophylactic devices, are easily cleaned off, and leave no stains. They do sometimes give a "tacky" feeling—a kind of friction that can occur once the liquid part of the lube has been rubbed into the skin. There are two remedies for this: Apply more lube; or sprinkle the area with water tossed off from your fingers (keep a bowl of water on your nightstand for this) or a "spritzer" similar to one you might use for plants. In most cases a little moisture will bring the lube back to life.

These lubes are *not* for massages. For that, use massage oils, which are made to be used over large expanses of the body and intended for external use only.

Water-based lubes can, of course, be used in the vagina, on the penis, or on the condom for vaginal or anal intercourse. In fact, for those who complain that a condom dulls the sensations of intercourse, a little lube will have you moaning another tune.

Lubes are also great to use on your hand for masturbation and mutual masturbation.

For anal sex, lubes are a must since the anus produces no natural lubricants whatsoever. And, of course, lubes can be used for any sex toys that are inserted, such as dildos, vibrators, or butt plugs. There are a couple of additional things to keep in mind that will make using lube more pleasant.

Put it in your hand first so that it can warm up, then apply it to your partner. Never put lube directly onto your partner's skin. It will most likely be cold and snap him or her out of the sexual zone. Also, don't put too much on at a time. "A little dab will do ya," especially as you get used to how much you and your partner are comfortable with.

Speaking of comfort, if you're too embarrassed to go to a sex shop to pick up a tube of lube, there are plenty of stores on the Internet that have a wide variety available. They are relatively inexpensive—and worth their price in pleasure.

For those who want to experiment with lubes and oral sex, there are also a number of edible products available in a variety of flavors.

The *Kama Sutra*, having been written and compiled in a patriarchal society, saw the woman on top in sex when "a woman sees that her lover is fatigued by constant congress" or "to satisfy the curiosity of her lover, or her own desire of novelty." It describes three woman-on-top postures:

1. *The Pair of Tongs*: "When the woman holds the lingam in her yoni, draws it in, presses it, and keeps it thus in her for a long time, it is called the 'pair of tongs.'" The *Kama Sutra* only describes this action of the vagina. Presumably it can be performed in any position, but perhaps optimally with the woman on top.

2. *The Top*: This posture is basically an inversion of the Turning Position, with two important differences: It is the woman on top, not the man; she is not lying on top of him, rather she is seated, with her feet on the outside of his hips. She turns from facing him to facing his feet. Some commentaries have warned that this position might actually do harm to the penis.

3. *The Swing*: In this posture the *Kama Sutra* says the man should lie on his back and then he "lifts up the middle part of his body." It might be easier and more pleasurable for him to remain flat or raise his upper torso, supporting himself on his outstretched arms, as the woman, her back to him, lowers herself onto his penis.

In the "supported" or standing positions we see images evocative of the sculptures and paintings decorating Indian temple walls. In these we also see how Indians' reputation for acrobatic sexual postures came to be.

1. *Suspended Congress*: In this posture the man supports himself against a wall, and supports the woman by joining his hands underneath her buttocks. She suspends

The Pair of Tongs

herself by throwing her arms around his neck, and putting her thighs alongside his waist. She places her feet on the wall and moves herself to and fro.

2. *The Congress of a Cow:* There are many postures that are named after the mating of animals—a few of them being the Congress of a Dog, the Forcible Mounting of an Ass, the Congress of a Cat, the Jump of a Tiger, the Pressing of an Elephant, the Rubbing of a Boar, the Mounting of a Horse. In these the *Kama Sutra* suggests that "the characteristics of the different animals should be manifested by acting like them," which goes to show you that this venerable book did regard making love with a sense of humor. (But if you take Vatsayayana's advice, be sure that you have thick walls!) In the Congress of the Cow the woman stands on her hands and feet (not her knees) and the man "mounts her like a bull." "At this time everything that is ordinarily done on the bosom should be done on the back," the *Kama Sutra* advises.

Favorite positions

I like the traditional man on top. Gives me more leverage and enables me to have a vaginal orgasm; doggie style is good for manipulation of the clitoris while the man enters you from the rear, and enables me to have another vaginal orgasm; me on top, also enables me to have a vaginal orgasm.   Ada, 29

Rear entry. Just seems to hit the right spot. Another favorite: one or both legs up in the missionary position.   Christopher, 32

I love being fucked from behind. I think it is the way the penis can reach far up into the pussy from this position. I like the missionary position, mainly because it makes me feel as if he is in control. I love being on my side also. I can play with my pussy while he is fucking me.   Angela, 38

666

Doggie style. I also love to be on top.   Lynette, 26

666

I like it on the side and from the sit-down position.   Amelia, 25

666

When I am really in the mood—on my back with my legs on my husband's shoulders. When not really in the mood—on my side with my leg raised.   Dorothy, 31

666

Woman on top. My hands are free to explore her breasts, vagina, clitoris, etc. I have better movement.   Brad, 30

666

Doggie style. Me on top of her, with her legs on my shoulders.   Alan, 29

666

I am a diehard fan of the missionary. It allows me to be quite mobile. I get to see the man's facial expressions, which adds to my pleasure. Basimah, 40

666

Male on top. Sitting cross-legged, with female on top. Female head off bed going toward the floor, pelvis up in the air. Male sitting in chair, female sits on top.   Jake, 36

666

Sideways.   Emily, 24

Doggie style because it allows for the utmost penetration and gives access to the G-spot. Woman on top because it allows for a woman to have a certain degree of control for penetration.   Gene, 38

🜲🜲🜲

One of my favorites is sitting on my fiancé's lap, facing him. It is similar to being on top, yet different because we are practically face to face (or his face in my breast), the angle is comfortable and immediate. Theresa, 27

🜲🜲🜲

Holding her up in the air facing me in front. From behind with her bent over a table. From behind with her facedown on the bed, butt angled up.   Howard, 38

🜲🜲🜲

Call me old-fashioned, but I like the missionary best.   Henrietta, 50

🜲🜲🜲

I would have to say my very favorite position is doggie style. This is because you can have the most intense orgasm this way. Or at least I can. Cindy, 30

🜲🜲🜲

We're standing up, and she's bent over. This is best because everyone feels like they are working equally.   Carlos, 24

🜲🜲🜲

Missionary position and mate entering vagina from behind while he is against my back. I like the closeness.   Donna, 33

🜲🜲🜲

Missionary position and me on top because I like to look at him. Lucy, 46

From the back . . . for more stimulation of the clitoris. . . . On top for the same reasons. . . .   Charlotte, 37

ⓖⓖⓖ

My legs on his shoulders while he's on top of me because it gets deeper, from the back with my butt cheeks spread because it gets deeper, with me on top of him kind of like stooping down because it gets deeper, him on top with my legs inside of his because he's then rubbing his penis up against my clit, and also the more he slides up the deeper it gets.   Sue, 25

C.A.T. Position

Talk about teaching an old dog new tricks. In a sense, that is what the C.A.T. Position is about—breathing new life into the position that has become the symbol of tried, true, and tired. But with the movement of an inch or two, the missionary, it is said, can deliver orgasms to the woman that will rock her world. It's simple to assume the C.A.T. position. First, get in the missionary position: man on top of the woman. Once the man enters the woman, he inches his way up so that the base of his penis rests on the woman's clitoris. But don't thrust. Rub, grinding the base of your penis against the woman's clitoris. Women have called this position a "slow burn" orgasm, one that gives a more "intense and intimate" release. But men need to be careful. One male sexual adventurer said, "My wife got into it, and so I tried to keep the

> An ingenious person should multiply the kinds of congress after the fashion of the different kinds of beasts and of birds. For these different kinds of congress, performed according to the usage of each country, and the liking of each individual, generate love, friendship, and respect in the hearts of women.
>
> —Kama Sutra

motion going. But I finally had to stop. All that pressure and grinding at that angle made me feel like my penis was going to snap at the base."

Ain't Nothin' but a G-Thang, Baby

Simply put, the G-spot is supposed to be the hot button that sends the woman into sexual orbit. Makes her a Roman candle. Lights her up. It is reputed to intensify sexual pleasure, especially orgasms, and can make some women multi-orgasmic. It is even said that the G-spot, touched at the right time in the right way, can stimulate female ejaculation, a spout of vaginal fluid from the female.

Some women claim not to have a G-spot. Others think they might have one but can't find it. The term came to the mass public in 1982 with the publication of a book called *The G Spot and Other Recent Discoveries About Human Sexuality* by John Perry and Beverly Whipple. The area was named after Dr. Ernst Grafenberg, who wrote about its location in a 1950 article. But prior to that it was not totally unknown. Two hundred years earlier, a Dutch anatomist said there was an area in the vagina that was similar in composition to a man's prostate and associated with sexual pleasure.

Fact, or the lurid imagination of sexually frustrated scientists—men who have been in their ivory towers too long? So far, studies have shown that virtually every woman has the spot, although it is not an erogenous zone for all. Want to see for yourself? First, make sure your bladder is empty. When the G-spot swells, it frequently stirs nerves that signal the need to urinate. But most women say that sensation soon passes, as the stimulation of the G-spot continues. Now move your finger about two inches into the vaginal canal and press upward toward the stomach. If you have a partner, lie on your back and have him insert his index finger into you, with his palm up and his finger crooked as if he is beckoning someone. In that motion he should feel a small spongy mass, and you might feel some shimmer—or more—of sexual pleasure. Make sure the vagina is well lubricated before doing this, and trim your fingernails; otherwise you risk hearing moans that are caused by something other than sexual pleasure.

The Big O

Sorry guys, but the vaginal orgasm, which has been considered the queen of orgasms since Freud first proclaimed it so in the late nineteenth century, is way overrated. In fact, it is virtually nonexistent. The vaginal orgasm's coronation as the orgasm sine qua non was a case of male-pattern arrogance. Experts wanted to say that women climaxed through sexual intercourse, the same way men do. It's not that clitoral orgasm was unknown, but it was considered childish, an infantile way of achieving pleasure. The so-called vaginal orgasm, arrived at through penetration, was seen as mature. For decades, it was the kind of orgasm any woman worth her salt sought. For decades, it was the kind of orgasm any woman worth her salt achieved, according to the pundits of the time.

Truth be told, most women do not orgasm because they've been penetrated by the almighty penis. At least, not the almighty penis unaided by some sort of prestidigitation—say, the woman or man massaging the woman's clitoris during penetration, or perhaps some hot and heavy groin-to-groin rubbing.

There are physiological reasons why the vaginal orgasm is a relatively rare phenomenon. First, while it is true that the largest human sexual organ is the brain, the only human body part devoted solely to sex is the clitoris. Nature put it there so that women can get off. The G-spot notwithstanding, (and a penis will seldom hit the G-spot during intercourse), trying to climax without touching the clitoris is like trying to give a man an orgasm by standing fifty paces from him and staring at his crotch. You aren't optimizing your chances for success. The best way to achieve an orgasm is through manual or oral stimulation on or around the clitoris. The location bears repeating: on *or* around the clitoris.

Men, don't think you are going to drive your woman wild by rubbing her clit as if you are cleaning a stain from your bathtub. Some women are very sensitive down there, and for them direct manipulation of the clitoris is painful. Your woman will be begging you to stop, but not for the reason you'd like. Some women prefer gentler and less direct stimulation of the clitoris or stimulation of the area around it through massage.

Clitoral contact is a perfect instance of when communication is essential to achieve maximum pleasure. It's also an instance of when a woman masturbating in front of her man might be a valuable lesson for him, not to mention an erotic experience for the both of them, if they are relaxed in one another's presence. (She can, of course, masturbate alone for pleasure and to get a sense of the kinds of stimulation her body responds best to.) In in-tandem lovemaking, the woman can show her lover how she likes to be touched—hard or soft, in circles or up and down, directly or indirectly, with a steady tempo or pressure, or with a tempo or pressure that increases in intensity. And so on. Even so, it's not as if a man can just memorize the woman's movement and moans, and go by rote from there. How she wants to be touched at a given time depends on her mood, the environment, the circumstances, where she is in her menstrual cycle. And so on. But at least he'll have a good start.

Speaking of moans and groans, this is as good a place as any to caution lovers: Don't give in to the tyranny of the orgasm. Like the famous ketchup, there are (at least) 57 varieties of orgasms for both men and women, although women seem to be more attuned to the full range, assuming they climax at all. Some orgasms are like Macy's Fourth of July fireworks; others are mellow fizzlers. Don't get bushwacked into thinking that they all must be like the explosions.

The other issue is the great orgasm hoax. Yes, even men fake it sometimes because they are tired and don't want to go on, or because what the women is doing is not very effective and it is one way to get her to stop. But with a little detective work, if she is so inclined, a woman can figure out if the man is faking. A women's faked orgasm, on the other hand, is more difficult to detect, and short of *When Harry Met Sally* histrionics, men are frequently reduced to asking. But asking can be inviting a kind of tyranny, because it assumes the preeminence of the orgasm, as if sex is worthless without it. For some, this may be the case. But for others, there can be intense sexual pleasure without a physiological orgasm. It's also possible for there to be physiological orgasm without a great deal of sexual pleasure. It all depends on the person, the situation, the partner they are with, and so forth.

Mare's Position/Kegel Exercises

The mare's position is less a position than a technique. In the words of the *Kama Sutra*, it occurs when the "woman forcibly holds in her yoni the lingam after it is in." The technique can be implemented in any number of sexual positions. This "milking" of the penis is achieved by tensing and relaxing the pelvic floor muscle, called the pubococygeus or PC muscle. This muscle is suspended between the genitals and the anus in both men and women, and pulsates during orgasm.

A physician, Dr. Arnold Kegel, is credited with creating exercises in the 1950s that are said to have a beneficial effect on those muscles, helping to curb problems with incontinence, contributing to vaginal tone before and after childbirth, and even leading to better orgasms. Typically, the way to initially find the PC muscle is to start and stop the flow when urinating. It is important not to use your leg, back, or buttock muscles in the process. Your anus should be relaxed, also. Sitting on the toilet with the legs apart helps to determine whether or not you are using only the PC muscle. For women, another method of finding the pelvic floor muscle is to lie on your back with your legs apart and insert a finger or two inside the vagina. Try to squeeze so that you feel the vagina clench around your fingers.

Once you have successfully isolated the pelvic floor muscle, you can begin the Kegel exercises, which are essentially sets of isometric exercises. Tense and relax the PC muscle (but not while urinating) to build control and strength. There are many variations. Here are some basics:

- Contract the pelvic muscles intensely for one second, then relax them. Do this ten times in a row, three times a day. Gradually increase the number of contractions so that by the end of one month you are doing ten contractions, twenty times a day.

- Vary the previous exercise by holding the contraction for a count of three, and then releasing. Mix the exercises up, some short and some long.

- Another method is to imagine the vagina as an elevator. Visualize the entrance of the vagina as the ground floor, with the top floor near the navel. Now, imagine moving an elevator up the vagina by slowly and deliberately contracting the muscles. When you get to the top, hold it. Try this twice daily. Or you might imagine that you are using your PC muscles to siphon water up into your vagina, drop by drop. Try this twice a day.

Kegel exercises can be done at any time: you can do sets of them while watching a television program or on the bus, while eating, and of course, when making love. (That's the Mare's position.) But be patient. Be consistent. Results do not happen overnight, but changes have been noted in as little as three weeks.

So let us not make that assumption that the partner needs an orgasm, much less multiple ones, to feel satisfied. It all comes down to communication—and requires both parties to take responsibility for their own sexual pleasure. Women, are you hearing what I'm telling you? If you want to climax, you should let your lover know, and if you have a preferred way of attaining that climax, let your lover know that, too. If a member of a couple is interested in intimacy, not just focused on the big O, it should be fine to say, "Tonight I simply want to make you happy."

Anal Sex

Although it is not addressed in the *Kama Sutra*, anal sex is increasingly referenced in mainstream modern American culture. It is to the late 20th and early 21st centuries what oral sex was to the mid 20th century: Forbidden. Shrouded in mystery. The object of humor, ridicule, and obsessive attention. There are an increasing number of books that sing the praises of various forms of anal sex, from penetration with the penis, a finger or two, a foreign object such as a dildo (but be sure the object has a flared base so that it doesn't inadvertently become lost in the rectum), and analingus, or licking the anus, also known by the slang expression, a "rim job." Part of this attention might be the taboo nature of anal sex, especially since there are fewer and fewer sexual taboos around. Part of its allure may be physiological. There are many nerves in the anus. For men, stimulation of the prostate can be pleasurable and in some instances lead to orgasm. Even women, who have no direct sexual organ there, have been known to have orgasm, whether from the sensation or from the sense of doing something that is taboo. If you are interested in experimenting with anal sex, these are the basic points to remember:

1. If you want to either give or receive anal sex (after all, a woman can use a dildo on her man), *talk about it* first. Nothing could spoil a potentially rewarding experience faster than an unannounced probe in the

caboose. Some men find the massaging of the prostate very pleasurable. Some women find they derive pleasurable sensations when the
penis is inserted so that it rubs up against the vaginal wall. Then again,
some men and women find those sensations uncomfortable. So talk
about what you might want to have done to you there. If you or your
mate are self-conscious, try joking about anal sex or use Internet sites
or erotica to lower inhibitions and make way for candid conversation.

2. Remember to bathe, preferably after the last bowel movement, if
not even closer to the act. Some authors suggest taking an enema an
hour or so before an expected anal encounter. If your last bowel
movement was at least an hour before your sex play, you should be in
good shape. Anal play is not necessarily nasty. Nonetheless, even if
you are part of a monogamous couple *always use protection* when engaging in anal sex. The anus and rectum, no matter how recently
washed, can harbor diseases that can be injurious if encountered by
the vagina or mouth. And the anus is likely to tear, even if ever so
slightly, creating an opportunity for an unhealthy mixing of bodily fluids and bacteria. So be sure to use a condom, and if performing
analingus, use a dental dam or at the very least a cellophane wrap.
And *never, ever* move your mouth, penis or dildo from the rectum to
the vagina, without a thorough cleansing.

3. *Go slowly.* Anal sex should not be painful. If you experience pain,
then you should stop. If you go slowly, you should have no problems

with this—*RELAX*. Relaxation will almost come automatically if you tend to the previous items: You'll have agreed to try the act; you won't have to worry about smells that might make you self-conscious; you won't have to worry about contracting a disease, even from a long-time monogamous loved one; and you will take your time and be able to digest the new sensations.

Favorite sex ever

I was really in love with my partner and it didn't matter what he did, just as long as it was him doing it.   Tamara, 24

🔯🔯🔯

With my then boss on the conference table. It was taboo and this made the passion intensify. I never felt that way before. He taught me to ask and get what I need sexually.   Aminah, 29

🔯🔯🔯

Pretty much just screwing all over the house all day long very fun, very satisfying, very tiring. We were very sore afterward and very happy. Ronald, 38

🔯🔯🔯

When I realized I loved my current boyfriend, I was able to give of my-self freely and that made the sex spectacular.   Bella, 26

🔯🔯🔯

On the back of my truck because we were under the stars and we were sneaking, so that made it even more exciting, because anybody could have seen us.   Virginia, 25

🔯🔯🔯

With a very patient man who made sure that I had multiple, multiple or-gasms. I mean oral, manipulation with his fingers . . . licking every inch of my back, going over every inch of my body several times, before he even considered penetration. . . . He was wonderful. . . . It was all done on my time. . . . Whatever I wanted I got.   Iman, 37

🔯🔯🔯

I took a woman, who I still think should be my wife, back home with me to the Bahamas. While we had had sex on the beach before, what made this time special was we were on my home island—Acklins. It is very re-mote, and at night wild ponies run along the beach, and mate as well. Hiram, 30

☙☙☙

My partner and I got together with another couple and had a foursome. It was awesome. We had gone to another couple's house after a party. The woman asked me to join her in the kitchen, where she told me she wanted to eat me. I agreed and we returned to the living room and be-gan dancing together. Before I knew it we began kissing and fondling each other. The guys were stunned, but very pleased. The guys joined in switching off fucking the two of us, then she and I would gang up on one of the guys while the other one watched. Oh, and we did have safe sex.   Helen, 38

☙☙☙

The best sex I have had is when the man really went out of his way to please me both emotionally and physically: oral sex, taking his time. . . . Having sex out in the rain in the park. That was pretty erotic.   Michelle, 29

☙☙☙

On an airplane crossing the Pacific Ocean at night, laying across several seats with my partner. Very enjoyable.   Enid, 42

☙☙☙

Making love after a cozy, friendly day; palling around with a significant other at his apartment with no kids around. Showering together the next day.   Sharon, 32

Postcoital Expressions

For most of us the completion of the sex act—or the act of making love—is followed by a warm calm. There are, of course, the physical changes: relaxation of the muscles, the slowing down of the heart, sometimes the trickle of perspiration that has beaded up all over our skin. But there is the mental aspect, also, and a reflection.

At the end of congress the lover . . . should eat some betel leaves, and the citizen should apply with his own hand to the body of the woman some pure sandalwood ointment, or ointment of some other kind. He should then embrace her with his left arm, and with agreeable words should cause her to drink from a cup held in his own hand, or he may give her water to drink. They can then eat sweetmeat, or anything else, according to their liking. . . . The lovers may also sit on the terrace of the palace or house, and enjoy the moonlight, and carry on an agreeable conversation. At this time, too, while the woman lies in his lap, with her face toward the moon, the citizen should show her the different planets, the morning star, the polar star, and the seven Rishis, or Great Bear. This is the end of sexual union—

—Kama Sutra

What is the best way to end a sexual session?

Watching a movie on television or VCR.   Samuel, 33

ⓖⓖⓖ

Listening to ballads.   Maria, 43

ⓖⓖⓖ

Cuddled in one another's arms, because it is a great time to explore intimacy.   Grace, 50

ⓖⓖⓖ

I love to eat.   Maura, 27

ⓖⓖⓖ

I like a drink.   Calvin, 25

ⓖⓖⓖ

If it was romantic—maybe in each other's arms. If it was "buck wild," go with the flow!   Alicia, 33

ⓖⓖⓖ

Ice cream.   Louise, 50

ⓖⓖⓖ

Falling asleep.   Gabriel, 30

ⓖⓖⓖ

A shower if things were extra sticky.   Kendra, 44

ⓖⓖⓖ

Getting some rest, in anticipation of the next encounter.   Winnie, 26

What is the purpose of sex?

To satisfy and release pressure.   Alice, 34

🔯🔯🔯

Connecting two people.   Russell, 28

🔯🔯🔯

Closeness, intimacy, fun, sleeping aid.   Elsie, 39

🔯🔯🔯

Sex is to channel strong, intense energy, to achieve an intense feeling of pleasure. Lovemaking is different, the ultimate goal is for two people to experience each other in a special experience that allows them to totally express their deepest feelings for one another.   Lorna, 25

🔯🔯🔯

To make me happy.   Terence, 26

🔯🔯🔯

A way to enjoy your partner in his or her entirety.   Georgia, 25

🔯🔯🔯

A way to ensure that each partner experiences ultimate pleasure. A way to ensure that your relationship grows and flourishes.   Ellen, 29

🔯🔯🔯

Sometimes it's just a physical release of stress, tension, etc. Sometimes it's for the pleasure of partners, sometimes it's for revenge, anger. It just depends.   Peter, 44

🔯🔯🔯

Ultimate in pleasure. Connecting to the spirit.   June, 42

🔯🔯🔯

To unite as one and please each other.   Pauline, 29

♊♊♊

Release and intimacy.   Edward, 44

♊♊♊

To express the love I have for a man in a physical and intimate form. I yearn to unite in exquisite passion with the man I love. And it is vitally important to me that I meet his needs for him to obtain the greatest and strongest orgasm possible.   Gloria, 41

♊♊♊

Release of pent-up energy.   Anna, 36

♊♊♊

Simple physical pleasure.   Brad, 30

♊♊♊

Showing your partner how much you care for them and wanting them to feel loved.   Emily, 24

♊♊♊

Sex allows for spiritual connectedness between two individuals. It creates a bond that goes beyond the physical.   Arthur, 30

♊♊♊

To pleasure each other.   Harriet, 27

♊♊♊

Fun, physical fun and relaxation.   Jake, 38

♊♊♊

Stress reliever. You're able to move better. Arthritis sufferers feel less pain when sexually active. Good sex can rid any female of depression. Annette, 50

To express to your partner how you feel. For a woman, having sex with her partner is something very special and only shared when she is sure he is "worthy of her goodies." It is also a way of releasing tension, some even say it is a good way to lose weight.   Frances, 30

∞∞∞

For me it's about rewarding my physical and spiritual self for having made it this far on the planet.   Michael, 40

∞∞∞

Making love, not sex: Creating intimacy; improving health/prolonging life; showing love, affection, and unity.   Justin, 20

∞∞∞

Release of tension.   Lucy, 46

∞∞∞

The ultimate purpose is to procreate . . . but I think the object of sex is to show a partner you love how much you love them. I don't think that sex should be performed outside the boundaries of love.   Charlotte, 37

∞∞∞

To relax for enjoyment. For bonding. A lot of things at different times. Virginia, 25

ACKNOWLEDGMENTS

It may take two to tango, but it takes a multiplicity of people to create a book. I am indebted to all those who have helped bring *SoulMates* to fruition. There is my agent, Sandra Dijkstra of the Sandra Dijkstra Literary Agency, whose belief in the book from the beginning buttressed my own confidence. There is Sandy's crack staff, Nicole Pitesa and Elisabeth James, who also provided support by lending an ear or a hand, for as long as needed, whenever needed.

And much gratitude to the folks at The Shark Bar in Manhattan who graciously allowed me to interview their customers.

I am also indebted to Neverne Covington who furnished the artwork for this illustrated guide, and to the Publicity and Marketing team at Plume: Brant Janeway, Abby Vinyard, Sarah Melnyk, Sarah Buntzman, and Doreen Davidson.

Thanks to Jeff Freiert, Phillip Wilentz, and Arthur Maisel for their hard work in shepherding this project through the production phases.

SoulMates wouldn't be at Plume if it weren't for Deirdre Mullane, who acquired it. Rosemary Ahern and Sara Bixler's suggestions were invaluable. Last, but not least, I am indebted to my editor, Gary Brozek, whose sharp eye, alert ear, and keen intelligence contributed so much to giving *SoulMates* its golden balance of steely fact and luminescent romance.

Author's Note

SoulMates is my latest book in the Before the Mayflower Project™ series. The purpose of The Project™ is to improve the circumstances of black Americans so that by 2019, the 400th anniversary of our first arrival to what is now the United States, we will have something to celebrate. The Project is based on the fact that no matter what our political, religious, or philosophical persuasion, we all want the same things: economic empowerment, responsible expression of sexuality, quality education—the list could easily go on. We may, however, go about achieving those goals in different ways, and that is the point of the Before the Mayflower Project: Unity of Purpose, Diversity of Means, and the Collective Will to achieve our goals by 2019. For more information about The Project™ and to print a copy of the Before the Mayflower Compact™, go to www.ericcopage.com

Other books in the Before the Mayflower Project are:

Kwanzaa: An African-American Celebration of Culture and Cooking
Black Pearls: Daily Meditations, Affirmations and Inspirations for
    African-Americans
Black Pearls for Parents
Black Pearls Journal
Black Pearls Book of Love
A Kwanzaa Fable
Soul Food: Inspirational Stories for African Americans

The CDs are:

Kwanzaa Music: A Celebration of Black Cultures in Song.
Kwanzaa Party: A Celebration of Black Cultures in Song.

Peace,
Eric V. Copage